More Glooscap Stories

LEGENDS OF THE WABANAKI INDIANS

More Glooscap Stories

LEGENDS OF THE WABANAKI INDIANS

by Kay Hill

ILLUSTRATED BY JOHN HAMBERGER

Reprinted in *Canadian Favourites* Edition 1988

Canadian Cataloguing in Publication Data

Hill, Kay, 1917-
   More Glooscap stories

(Canadian favourites)
ISBN 0-7710-4089-X

1. Abnaki Indians – Legends – Juvenile literature.
2. Indians of North America – Legends – Juvenile
literature.   I. Hamberger, John.   II. Title.

PS8515.I44M67 1978   j398.2'097   C78-006650-2
PZ7.H544Mo 1978

Printed and bound in Canada

McClelland and Stewart
The Canadian Publishers
481 University Avenue, Toronto, Ontario,
M5G 2E9

To Margaret and Chris

Contents

CONTENTS

Glossary

PRONUNCIATION	IDENTIFICATION
Ableegumooch — Ab-lee-ga-mooch'	the Rabbit
Abukcheech — Ah-book'-cheech	the Mouse
Abukchelo — Ah-book'-chee-lo	the Skunk
Akilinek — Ah-kill'-ee-neck	country of the Red Giants
Blomidon — Blom'-ah-dun	home of Glooscap
Booöin — Boo-oh'-in	a wizard
Bootup — Boo-tup'	the Whale
Chenoo — She-noo'	a cannibal giant
Chepitkam — Shep'-it-kam	a horned serpent
Coolnajoo — Cool-nah'joo	foolish one
Culloo — Cull-oo'	large mythical bird
Elaak — Ee-lay'-ack	name meaning "harmful"
Kakakooch — Kah-kah'-kooch	the Crow
Keewasu — Kee-wah'-soo	the Muskrat
Kekwajoo — Kee-kwah'-joo	the Badger
Keoonik — Kee-oo-nik'	the Otter

GLOSSARY

Keskamzit — Kess-kam'-sit	magic power
Keskum — Kess'kum	the Frost Giant
Kespak — Kess'-pack	a name
Kespeadooksit — Kess-pee-ay-dook'-sit	"the story ends"
Kitpooseagunow — Kit-poose-ee-ay-goo'-now	name meaning "one born after his mother's death"
Kobit — Koh'-bit	the Beaver
Kogun — Koh'gun	name meaning "froth on the water"
Kookoogwes — Koo-koo'-gwess	the Owl
Kookwes — Kook-ways'	giant or giants
Kukwu — Cue'-kwah	earthquake
Kwah-ee — Kwah'-ee	hail! (Indian greeting)
Kweemoo — Kwee'-moo	the Loon
Lox — Locks	the Indian devil
Madooes — Mah-doo'-ees	the Porcupine
Malicetes — Mah'-lah-seets	Indians
Malsum — Mahl'-soom	the Wolf
Masu — Mah'-soo	a name
Meejeedayjick — Mee-jee-day'-jick	name of a wizard
Megumoowesoos — Mee-gum-a-wee'-soos	Little People; halfway people
Menaagan — Men-ah'-gun	a name
Micmacs — Mick'-macks	Indians
Miko — Mee'-ko	the Squirrel
Moalet — Moh-ah-let'	one who lives off his neighbors
Mooin — Moo'-in	the Bear
Moonumkweck — Moon-um'-kweck	the Woodchuck
Munagesunook — Mun-ag-ah-soo'-nook	Anticosti Island
Nabeskus — Nah-bess'-kuss	a name

Nesoowa — Ness'-oo-wah	a name
Noogumee — Noo-ga-mee'	grandmother
Oolastuk — Oo-lass'-took	St. John River
Oona — Oo'nah	a name
Ooteomul — Oo-tay'-oh-mull	Glooscap's kettle
Passamaquoddies — Pass-ah-mah-quod'-ees	Indians
Penobscots — Pen-ob'-scots	Indians
Pipsolk — Pip'-sock	a name
Pitou — Pee-too'	a name
Pulowech — Poo-lah'-weck	the Partridge
Pulwaugh — Pool-wah'	a name
Sabadis — Sah-bah'-dees	a name
Sakum — Sah-koom'	name of Chief's wife
Skadegamooch — Skah-dah-gah-mooch'	a ghost
Team — Tee-am'	the Moose
Teetees — Tee-tees'	the Blue Jay
Teymumkwak — Tey-mum'-quack	the Wild Goose
Toma — Toe-mah'	a name
Tomik — Toe'-meek	a name
Wasek — Wass'-eck	a name
Wasis — Wah'-sees	baby
Wejebok — Wedge-ee'-bock	a name
Wejosis — Wee-joe'-siss	a name
Welahe — Well-ah'-ee	a name
Welowna — Well-oh'-nah	a name
Winsit — Win'-sit	name of an evil Chenoo
Wiskum — Wiss'-koom	a name
Wokun — Wah-koon'	a name
Wokwes — Wok'-wees	the Fox
Wokwotoonok — Walk-wah-too'-nock	the North Wind
Woltes — Wall'-tays	a name

Glooscap, the Great Chief

WHEN THE Indian storytellers speak of the Old Time, they mean long ago, long before the White Man knew their country, when at first there was only the forest, the sky, and the sea—no living creatures. Then, so the legends say, Glooscap came. He came from the Sky in a stone canoe with Malsum, his twin brother.

The two were giants twelve feet tall and both could make themselves larger at will. By means of magic belts, they could transform nature and bear the hottest heat, the coldest cold. Glooscap was manlike, but Malsum had the head of a wolf. In other more important ways, they were different. Glooscap, the good and powerful Chief, had come to people the land with men and animals. Malsum, banished from Skyland for his evil ways, had been sent to redeem himself in Glooscap's service. Yet, alas, he was jealous of his brother and meant, if he could, to kill Glooscap and become Chief in his place.

Down out of the sky floated the great stone canoe bearing the giants. Landing and anchoring where the sun rises, the canoe turned into an isle which today we call Newfoundland. Its woods and lakes and lovely rivers were peaceful and this was Glooscap's home for a long while.

He set to work. First, out of the rocks he made the small, halfway people—the *megumoowesoos*—and sent them to dwell in rocky caves. From among them, he chose Marten to be his servant and friend, and the world was suddenly a brighter place. The Great Chief smiled with the joy of creation, but Malsum's heart was bitter at not having his brother's power to make good things. Next, Glooscap made men by shooting arrows into the trunks of ash trees. Out of the trees stepped men and women with shining black hair, and he named them Wabanaki—those who live in the dawn, or where the sun rises. He chose one to keep his lodge and the name he gave her, Noogumee, was ever afterward a Wabanaki name of respect for elderly women. Gazing on his handiwork, Glooscap's shout of triumph shook the topknots of the tallest pines—but Malsum scowled.

Finally, out of clay, Glooscap made the animals. He had made Miko the squirrel, Team the moose, Mooin the bear, and many, many others when, secretly, Malsum touched his belt and whispered an evil charm. The last of the clay in Glooscap's hands twisted of itself and fell to the ground, where it came to life as a strange animal—not badger, not beaver, not wolverine, but something of all three, a creature as restless and wild as its maker.

"His name is Lox!" said Malsum. "I made him!"

"So be it," said the Great Chief. "Let Lox live with us in peace."

But Malsum said to Lox privately, "You must stir up trouble for Glooscap wherever you can."

Now the Great Chief had made all the animals very large, much larger and stronger than men, and in this Lox saw his opportunity. He went in his beaver shape to Abukcheech the mouse, who was in those days the size of a bear, and said, "What great teeth you have. If you met a man, you could kill him with one bite."

"So I could!" said Abukcheech, and looked about for a man to bite.

"No, no, Abukcheech!" The Great Chief had heard and, touching his belt, he caused the mouse to become as tiny as he is today, able only to gnaw and nibble.

Then Lox went in his badger shape to Wokwes the fox, who was then as big as a tiger, with a hard uplifted tail. "What a magnificent tail that is, Wokwes. With it you could knock down trees."

"I certainly could!" said Wokwes, and down went the trees, but suddenly Glooscap was there, stroking his back, and the fox became the size he is today, with a soft bushy tail streaming out behind him.

Next, as a wolverine, Lox went to Kobit the beaver, who was a giant in those days, and said, "Kobit, you work all day damming up ponds for the benefit of others. Why don't you enjoy yourself for a change?"

"I will!" said the beaver. Diving and swimming about in the brooks, he stirred up the water and made it too muddy for fishing. Glooscap, seeing what had happened, cleared the water and made Kobit his present size.

And so it went—Lox stirring up the animals to make mischief, the Great Chief reducing them in size and power —until at last, losing patience, Glooscap summoned all the animals and warned them. "I have made you man's equal, but it seems you wish to become his master. Take care, or he may become yours."

The animals muttered angrily among themselves. "It is clear that as long as Glooscap is master, we can do nothing. Malsum would let us do as we please. If we had the Indians to help us, we could overthrow Glooscap!" But the Wabanaki were too busy fishing and gathering food to join in the troublemaking.

So Lox had to think of something else. He knew that both giants bore charmed lives and that neither could be killed except in one certain way. What that way was, each kept secret from all but the Stars, who were their brothers.

4

Lox soon noticed how each of the giants talked at times, privately, to the people of the Sky.

"Little does Malsum know," said Glooscap, thinking himself alone in the starlight, "that I can never die, unless struck in the heart by a flowering rush." And not far off, the wolf-headed Malsum muttered, "I am safe, for nothing can harm me but a fern root piercing my throat, and this Glooscap does not know."

Overhearing, Lox saw how he could turn things to his own ends. He went to Malsum in his beaver form and asked what he would give to know Glooscap's life secret.

"Anything!" cried Malsum. "What is it?"

The traitor told him. "Now give me a pair of wings that I may fly." But Malsum laughed scornfully.

"What good are wings to a beaver?" And kicking Lox out of his way, he sped to find a flowering rush. Furious, Lox hurried to Glooscap.

"Master, Malsum knows your secret and is about to kill you. He will die only if his throat is pierced by a fern root!"

Glooscap had barely torn the root from the ground, when Malsum appeared, flowering rush in hand. Touching their belts, both grew in a flash so tall their heads touched the clouds. Ah, what a battle that was! The sight of it was like flashing lightning, the sound of it like rolling thunder. Each blow made the earth tremble and the pine trees shake at their roots. So huge were the giants, they

5

fought both in Newfoundland and the Gaspé peninsula, a foot in either country, the Gulf of St. Lawrence a mere puddle between them! At last Malsum risked all in a mighty thrust but, stubbing his toe on an island, he lost his balance. Swift as light, Glooscap's fern root pierced the wolflike throat, and Malsum died—turning, as he fell, into a mountain on the coast of Gaspé.

Then the Indians shouted for joy, but the animals slunk off—all but Lox who came to Glooscap and said, "I'll have my reward now, Master, a pair of wings!"

"Faithless creature!" the Great Chief thundered. "*I* made no such bargain. Begone!" And he hurled stone after stone at the fleeing Lox, and where the stones fell in Minas Basin they turned into islands which are there to this day. The banished Lox, however, still roams the world stirring up trouble wherever he goes.

Now even though he had won the battle, Glooscap was sad. He had killed a brother, and he knew that every act both good and bad, for whatever reason, had good and bad consequences. As the mountain rose in Malsum's place, a rocky passage opened therein, letting in from the Outer World all manner of strange beings—*kookwes* or giants, both evil and good; wizards and sorcerers called *boooïns*; great Culloo birds strong enough to carry off whole families of men to their nests in the sky; the terrible *Chenoos* who were cannibals with hearts of ice; horned dragons such as the famous *chepitkam;* also witches, demons and

7

serpents, and the spirits of Wind and Famine and Frost and Storm. Rushing in all directions, they hid themselves until it would be their whim to fall on man. The world was no longer an empty and peaceful place.

Glooscap saw with sadness that he could not now return to his brothers in Skyland, but must remain and protect the Wabanaki, at least until they were able to defend themselves. He called his people around him and promised that if they would face their future trials with courage and energy, he would be their Chief and help them all he could.

Now he showed the people how to make bows and arrows and stone-tipped spears, and how to use them. "I made the animals to be man's friends, but they have acted with treachery. Hereafter they will be your servants." He showed the women how to scrape hides and make them into warm clothing, taught them how to make birchbark wigwams and canoes, to construct weirs to catch fish, and how to identify plants useful for medicine. "You have power now over even the largest wild creatures. Yet I charge you to use this power gently. If you take more game than you need, or kill for the love of killing, you will be visited by the giant Famine, by whose hand you will surely die."

He called Kweemoo the loon and appointed him his messenger. He took two wolves—one white for Day, one black for Night—and trained them to be his dogs. Finally, he called to Marten to launch his canoe, and signed to

Noogumee to bring food for the journey. The people, seeing he was about to leave them, cried out with dismay.

"I am not going far," he reassured them. "I must dwell in a separate lodge, in a high place from which I may watch over you no matter where you go." He stepped into the canoe. "Whoever seeks me diligently in time of need will find me."

And waving farewell, Glooscap and his companions sailed west to the mainland and into the Bay of Fundy which lies between the Maine-New Brunswick coast and the peninsula of Nova Scotia. There on a red and green headland known today as Blomidon, Glooscap built his lodge.

And while he dwelt there, many of his Indians also crossed to the mainland, peopling the eastern woodlands from Gaspé to Cape Cod, and forming themselves into many tribes—Micmacs, Malicetes, Penobscots, Passamaquoddies, and others—and during that time the Great Chief did many wonderful things for his people, of which you will hear in the pages to follow.

For the present, however, *kespeadooksit,* which means "the story ends."

The Rabbit
Makes a Match

ABLEEGUMOOCH the rabbit is a sociable creature, a little boastful perhaps, but kindhearted. So, when he saw his friend Keoonik the otter looking miserable, he wanted to know at once what was the matter and was there anything he could do. Well, it turned out that what the otter wanted was to get married. He wanted to marry Nesoowa, the daughter of Pipsolk; and the girl-otter was willing, but her father was not.

"Why not?" asked the rabbit, eying his friend. "You may not be the handsomest fellow in the world, Keoonik (otters can't compare with rabbits in looks), or the smartest (the rabbits are that), but you're honest and good-tempered and I dare say you'd provide quite a good living for a wife. Did you try anointing Pipsolk's head with bear grease?" This was the Indian way of asking if Keoonik had tried flattery on the girl's father.

"It wasn't any good," said Keoonik. "He thinks so well of himself already, nothing I could say would please him."

"How about a gift to sweeten his opinion?"

"No good. It isn't meat or presents he cares for—it's breeding and ancestors, and I haven't got any according to him." Keoonik added glumly—"I'm just an ordinary everyday kind of otter, not good enough for his daughter."

"Ah, Keoonik," sighed the rabbit, "there are many like Pipsolk, full of silly pride. (Pride—that's one thing rabbits haven't!) Look, my friend, since I am known everywhere as the wittiest and most persuasive Wabanaki in Glooscap's world, wouldn't you like me to have a talk with Pipsolk?"

"What sort of talk?" asked Keoonik.

"I could tell him what a good fellow you really are and how much better it would be to have a decent son-in-law with no relatives than a bad one with too many!"

"Tell him I'm very fond of Nesoowa, and would try to make her happy."

"I'll tell him," said the rabbit, and off he went.

Ableegumooch found Pipsolk and his numerous family sliding happily down a muddy slope near their home on the lake. This is a favorite pastime of otters.

"Step over here, will you, Pipsolk," called the rabbit from a drier spot up the bank. "I'd like to talk with you about Nesoowa."

11

Pipsolk excused himself to his family and stepped over. "What about Nesoowa?"

"Isn't it time she was married?" queried Ableegumooch, "to a kind and hard-working husband? I don't know if it's occurred to you, but good husbands don't grow on blueberry bushes. And remember, with Nesoowa off your hands, you will have fewer mouths to feed."

"Very true," agreed Pipsolk, "but a man must do the best he can for his daughter. What kind of father would I be if I passed her over to the first common sort who came along? Tell me, Ableegumooch, who were your people?"

"Eh?"

"Your ancestors. Were they important? Were they well-bred?"

The rabbit stuck out his chest.

"Pipsolk," he said complacently, "my family is one of the best. I have a long and noble ancestry, with notables on every branch of the family tree since the days before the light of the sun."

"H'mm," Pipsolk nodded thoughtfully. "Can you show proof of your aristocratic background?"

"Certainly. Haven't you noticed how I always wear white in the winter time? That's the fashion of the aristocracy."

"Really? I didn't know that. But what about your split lip, Ableegumooch? It doesn't indicate anything common, does it?"

"On the contrary, it's a sign of breeding. In my circles,

12

we always eat with knives, which is the polite way of feeding. One day my knife slipped, which is how my lip was damaged."

"But why is it your mouth and your whiskers keep moving even when you're still? Is that high style too?"

"Of course. You see, it's because I'm always meditating and planning great affairs. I talk to myself rather than to anyone of lesser quality. That's the way we gentlemen are!"

"I see. One more question. Why do you always hop? Why don't you walk like other people?"

"All my aristocratic forebears had a gait of their own," the rabbit explained loftily. "We gentle folk don't run like the vulgar."

"I'd no idea you were so well-bred, Ableegumooch," said Pipsolk. "Very well. You may have her."

The rabbit had opened his mouth to say something more about his aristocratic forebears, but now he closed it.

"I don't as a rule approve of marrying outside the tribe, but circumstances alter cases. Welcome, son-in-law."

Ableegumooch felt as though he had accidentally walked under an icy waterfall. He—to be married—and to an otter girl! The rabbit had never even thought of getting married! He opened his lips to say so, and hesitated, his whiskers twitching. Pipsolk was a man one didn't offend if one could help it. Many of his kind had a short way with rabbits! Moreover, the thought of marriage was rather pleasant, once one began to think about it. A pretty girl adds a nice touch to a wigwam. Besides, his grandmother was getting old and would be glad of help in the lodge.

He thought briefly of Keoonik, and worded an explanation silently in his mind. "I'm sorry, friend, but I didn't plan it this way, you know. I don't see how I can get out of it. Can I help it if Nesoowa's father wants the best for his daughter? You'll understand, I'm sure."

That night, Pipsolk invited all his relatives and friends to a feast and announced the engagement of Nesoowa to the well-known and aristocratic Ableegumooch, the marriage to take place at the end of the usual probationary period. It was customary among the Wabanaki of that time for a young man to provide for the family of his future bride for one year to show that he was capable of getting food and necessities for a wife and family. Keoonik was of course among the guests and, hearing the dreadful news, he could hardly believe his ears. He gave his faithless friend a long, bitter look as he left the party, and it quite shriveled Ableegumooch for the moment.

The rabbit tried to find excuses for himself. "It wasn't my fault. It's too late now, anyway, to back down."

So he set up a lodge near Pipsolk's and brought over his grandmother, who complained bitterly at having to move to such a damp place near all those noisy otters, but the rabbit paid no attention. His mind was wholly occupied with the problem of feeding those otters. He knew it would

14

be different from feeding himself and his grandmother. Rabbits live in meadows and forest undergrowth and are satisfied with herbs and grasses and tender twigs. Otters, on the other hand, live in or near water and like fish and frogs and salamanders for dinner. If Ableegumooch was to keep those otters fed, he must learn to be at home in the water, and a rabbit is not the best in the world when it comes to swimming. In fact, to be plain about it, of all swimmers and divers the rabbit is the very worst.

"Can you swim?" asked the young otters, with interest.

"Well—not yet," said Ableegumooch, adding cheerfully, "but I can learn." Ableegumooch is always willing to try.

He put his nose to the water. It smelled dank and weedy, not at all nice. He dipped one toe in the water to test its temperature—ugh, cold! He pulled his toe out again. After a good deal of sighing and dipping in and dipping out, the rabbit finally got himself into the water chest-deep and began to move his front paws in an awkward swimming motion. The watching otters nudged each other and chuckled. Then the rabbit tried to let go with his back feet, but sank at once and had to scramble in a panic to find solid ground again.

Nevertheless he kept trying, and after a whole day of failing and trying again, he managed to move a few strokes from shore, and all the otters applauded. Ableegumooch felt quite proud of himself, though he couldn't understand why the otters laughed even as they cheered.

Next he must learn to fish, they said.

"Fish? Well, I can try."

Pipsolk was already fretting about the fact that it was long past his usual dinner time.

"Patience," said the rabbit, trying to recall how otters fished. They dived first. Yes, that was the hard part. It meant ducking one's head right under the water. Never mind, if an otter could do it, so could a rabbit. And he ducked his head in the manner of otters and muskrats, hoisting his other end high up in the air so the little round tail would follow him down under the waves. Once upside down, with water in his nose and his ears and his eyes, the rabbit thought only of getting up to the surface again. He came up choking and spluttering, and oh didn't the air taste good!

"This way of fishing," he decided, "is not for me. Now, let me see, how do the bears go about it? I think they catch fish by just scooping them out of the water. I can do that, surely." So, standing in water up to his chin, Ableegumooch reached for a leaping frog, made a swipe at a devil's-darning-needle, grabbed at a trout flashing by—and missed all three, to the vast merriment of the otter family. Still the rabbit kept trying. He saw a fat insect alight on the branch of an Indian Pear Tree and at the same time a salmon swam into view. Trying to grab both at the same time, Ableegumooch stepped off into deep water and sank. Down he went and at the very bottom his long hind foot caught in a pile of brush. There he was held fast. In a dreadful panic, he kicked and twisted, trying to get free. As he fought, a brown shape flashed past him underwater, turned and came back. It was Keoonik!

Seeing his guilt clearly for the first time, Ableegumooch was sure the otter had come to take his revenge. Well, thought the rabbit, I suppose I deserve to die, but I'm not going to if I can help it—certainly not to please Keoonik! So he braced himself for one last effort, and at the same moment his foot was miraculously freed. He shot up to the surface, more than half-drowned, where Keoonik grabbed him and pushed him in no gentle fashion to the shore.

"False friend! Traitor!" growled the otter. "I ought to have left you there to perish!"

"Why didn't you?" gasped the rabbit, still coughing up water.

"Because drowning's too good for you," Keoonik grinned. "I'm waiting to see what Pipsolk does when he finds out he and his family must go hungry to bed tonight! Ah well—you'll make a good substitute, Ableegumooch. We otters are very fond of rabbit stew."

"I'm sorry I spoiled things for you with Nesoowa."

"You didn't," laughed the other. "Nesoowa says she will run away with me rather than marry you." Keoonik glanced hurriedly over his shoulder. "Here comes Pipsolk now, and he looks hungry! You'd better start running!"

After one look at Pipsolk's face, Ableegumooch would have been glad to take Keoonik's advice, but he couldn't. He was still too weak and breathless to run anywhere— and in such a strait, as usual, he thought of the Great Chief and whispered a plea for help.

Suddenly Glooscap—who comes as the wind comes and no man knows how—stood between Ableegumooch and the wrathful otter.

"Boasting again, Ableegumooch," said the Great Chief, who probably loved the rabbit best of all his creatures,"and see where it's got you!"

"I'm sorry to bother you, Master," the rabbit apologized. "It was sink or swim—and I've already tried swimming!"

Glooscap shook his head in despair, trying not to smile. He turned to the otter, who was now looking innocent, as if rabbit stew had never entered his mind.

"Pipsolk, I want you to forget all about breeding and background and such nonsense and just tell Ableegumooch frankly what you think of him as a son-in-law."

Pipsolk turned to the rabbit.

"The fact is, Ableegumooch, you may be good enough in your way, but your breeding and ancestors won't fill my children's mouths. You'll never do as a husband for my daughter. She would soon starve. Indeed, after experiencing your kind of son-in-law, I can see more virtue in Keoonik's sort. I believe, if Nesoowa is willing, I shall give him a trial after all."

"There!" cried Ableegumooch. "I told you I'd help you, Keoonik." But the otter had rushed away to find Nesoowa and tell her the good news.

Glooscap gave his rabbit a severe look. "I hope you have learned something from all this, Ableegumooch."

"Oh, I have," cried the rabbit. "I know now I'm not cut out for swimming and fishing. From now on, I shall be satisfied just to be what I am, the handsomest, the cleverest, and best-bred rabbit in the world! And—" as an afterthought, "the best matchmaker!"

Whereupon to the rabbit's surprise Glooscap began to laugh, and he laughed so hard that all the trees bent with the gust of his laughter, and Ableegumooch had to cling to the Master's leg to keep from being blown away.

And there, *kespeadooksit,* our tale ends.

Wejosis and the
Wind Giant

Long ago in the Old Time, there were giants—the Indians called them *kookwes*—and one of the most dreaded of them was Wokwotoonok, the North Wind. This *kookwes* hated people, especially children, and wanted to destroy them all.

One day he set out to do that very thing!

It was Indian Summer, the warm time that often comes in the Fall after the real summer is over. The days were growing short and the Micmacs went out one fine day to fish. Knowing and fearing Wokwotoonok this time of year, they also knew that he dwelt far away in the North and while he stayed there the earth would be quiet and the sea peaceful. The Indians fished with spears for cod and mackerel, and were too absorbed at first to notice the first slight riffle of wind on the water.

21

Then suddenly the waves began to rise and the spray to fly, the canoes to rock and ship water. Fishing was forgotten. The Indians seized their paddles and headed for shore, but with a howl of glee Wokwotoonok swept down on them, smashing their frail craft and flinging them into the sea where all were drowned.

On shore, the children stood frozen with horror. The flowers and grass around them began to sway and flatten. The sea birds screamed and swooped out of the *kookwes'* path, and the waves dashed themselves wildly against the rocky shore. "Prepare to die!" howled the giant. "I am Wokwotoonok the wind giant and all who stand in my way shall perish!"

The children woke at last to their danger and turned to flee, but there was nowhere to go that the *kookwes* could not follow. Then Wejosis, a boy quicker-witted than the rest, shouted to the younger children—"Follow me!"

"Stop!" shouted the giant, "you cannot escape"—but the children obeyed Wejosis and followed as fast as they could to a cave along the shore. The boy hurried them inside, then turned to close the entrance with a huge boulder, but now the wind was nearly upon him. He could feel the giant's breath as he pushed and pulled with all his might and at last the great stone began to move, rolling across the cave's mouth just as Wokwotoonok hurled himself against it.

Inside, the children huddled together, trembling, while

the giant pushed with all his strength against the boulder, but the rock stood firm.

"You can't stay in there forever!" the baffled *kookwes* shouted. "Some day I shall come upon you when you are not looking!" And then he turned and blew sullenly away to his home in the North.

Now the children were safe, for a while at any rate. It was true they could not stay in the cave forever. There was nothing in there to eat, no water to drink, no blankets to keep them warm—and now they remembered they had no parents to take care of them any more. Wejosis did his best to comfort and encourage the weeping children. "It is useless to cry. We must not waste our strength in despair. We will learn now to take care of ourselves!" And he told them to lie down and rest. While they slept, Wejosis thought about what they must do next day.

When dawn came, he led them out of the cave. Trees lay flat on the earth, torn out by the roots. All the wigwams had blown away and the food was lost among the debris washed up by the ocean. The air was still again, however. There was no sign of Wokwotoonok.

Wejosis took command. He told the smallest children to gather wood for the fires. "The rest must hunt for food. Some of you dig for clams where you see holes in the wet sand. Others try to find some late berries and roots which may be good to eat—but don't go far in case the giant comes back."

23

The children did as Wejosis told them and soon there was food for all. But what next? The clams would soon give out, and there were few berries left so near the shore. Wejosis saw that they must risk leaving the shelter of the cave to go farther inland where the forest would protect them and provide food. So he gathered them all together and led them toward the trees. While they were still some distance off, they heard the voice of Wokwotoonok—"Ah-hah! I have you now!"

"Run!" cried Wejosis.

The children needed no urging. Fear put wings to their feet and they reached the forest just as the wind *kookwes* reached it.

"I've got you this time," roared Wokwotoonok. "Don't think you can hide, for I shall rip those trees up by the roots, and scatter them far and wide!"

But the hardwood trees of the forest—the maples, the elms, the chestnuts, and oaks—were not high and thin like those on the shore. They were wide and bushy and grew close together, sheltering each other. As the children scuttled under them, the trees prepared to fend off the giant. They lowered their thick branches over the children and clung to the earth with their tough roots. Wokwotoonok leaned against them, pushed here, prodded there, but he could not reach the children.

Muttering with rage, he gave up the search at last and went away.

The children crept from their hiding places, thanking the trees for their protection.

Wokwotoonok, however, had not given up. He had decided to seek an ally—Keskum, the frost giant. Keskum was strong too, cold of heart and vain of his power.

"We must first kill the trees," decided Wokwotoonok. "Then I can get at the children."

The frost *kookwes* shrugged disdainfully. "It is not necessary to kill the trees—merely destroy the leaves." He added with a crackle of vainglorious pride, "I can cause the sap to freeze, if you like, so the leaves will die and turn brittle. Then you need only blow them away!"

"Then let us be off!" cried the wind *kookwes*.

The two sped off to the land of the Micmacs.

The hardwood trees saw them coming and felt a chill of fear. "Hurry!" they told Wejosis."Lead the children under those other trees—quickly!" Then the elms, the beeches, the oaks, the chestnuts, and maples braced themselves for the onslaught of the two giants.

Keskum came upon them first, driving his icy crystals into their trunks and branches, freezing the sap inside, turning the leaves dry and brittle. Then came Wokwotoonok, breathing his cold breath upon them in hate and triumph. Branches were tossed about and leaves scattered, and soon every tree was stripped bare. They stood cold and lonely, their leaves spread over the hard ground, but the wind giant was struck with amazement. Where were the children? At last his eye fell on the evergreens—the spruce, the pine, the fir, and the hemlock—their needles still firm and green, and he knew the children were safe under their branches. He turned on Keskum.

"Why do you not use your boasted power against those trees?"

"I have no power over the evergreens. It's no use blaming

me. Our father, the Sun, designed them to remain green and full of life all year."

"Then what good are you to me?" asked Wokwotoonok disgustedly, and he went back to his cave in the North and sulked there for a long time, while Keskum went his own way.

But still the children were in danger. Wejosis was old enough to remember that each year about this time the Ice King came to the land of the Wabanaki. It would be impossible to sleep on the ground when winter came, and where would they find food, or wigwams to cover them?

"Build a fire of green wood," said Wejosis, making up his mind it was time they had help. "Then bring me some spruce boughs—thick ones."

When the fire was going, Wejosis laid the boughs on top, then lifted them. A puff of smoke rose in the still sky. Again he laid the boughs down and lifted them rapidly three times. The resulting smoke spelled this message in the sky—"Help! Glooscap!"

Now all this unhappy time, the Great Chief had been busy elsewhere and had not noticed that his Micmacs were in trouble. Reading the smoke signals, he rushed to their aid, and learned how the children had lost their parents, how the giants Wokwotunook and Keskum had pursued them, and how they feared the new *kookwes,* Winter.

How could he make the children safe again? He could

27

not bring back their parents, for they were in the happy hunting grounds in the sky and would not return. He could not keep the Ice King away, for he had once given his word that Winter would have power over the land for half the year. He could, however, provide foster parents for the children and this he did at once, shooting arrows into the ash trees and bringing forth full-grown Indians to care for the orphans. He knew the children would be cherished by these foster parents, for Indians love adopted children as well as their own. Yet the children still looked unhappy.

"What more can I do?" asked Glooscap, wanting very much to see them smile.

Wejosis spoke for all.

"The trees—they saved us, and in doing so, they died. Can you bring them back to life again?"

"They are not really dead," the Great Chief told them, "only frozen in a kind of sleep. In the Spring, they will awake and grow new leaves."

Wejosis looked at the poor dead leaves on the ground.

"Not *those* leaves," he said sorrowfully. "Not the leaves that saved us from the giants."

Glooscap sat down and smoked his pipe thoughtfully. "I cannot put the leaves back on their branches," he said at last, "but I'll tell you what I *can* do!" Now in that time there were no little forest birds in the land of the Wabanaki, for Glooscap had not yet thought to make them. Of course there were the sea birds—Gull, Wild Goose, Kingfisher and so on—but they were wild and lived on the ocean. There were no birds to be company for the children, to give pleasure with their pretty feathers and happy songs. And this was Glooscap's plan—"I shall take the fallen leaves," he said, "and change them into birds!"

The children smiled.

Glooscap touched his belt briefly and at once a flock of little birds sprang up and began to sing. There were robins and thrushes, brown and red like the leaves of the

oak. There were finches and hummingbirds, yellow and green like the alder and willow. There were scarlet tanagers and orioles and grosbeaks, like the red, gold, and bronze of the maple leaves. And they were beautiful!

"Now," said Glooscap, "I have made the birds and I give you children charge over them—to protect them as you were protected by the leaves from which they are sprung."

Joyously, the children promised that they and their children and their children's children would always watch over the small birds and keep them safe from harm.

And so—*kespeadooksit*—the story ends.

Kespak and the Caribou

ONE DAY LONG AGO, in the time of the Old People, a Passa-maquoddy boy named Kespak asked his father why he had been given a name meaning "last son" when there was no child in the wigwam but himself.

The father sighed deeply.

"There was one before you, my son," the father said, "your elder brother, Masu. He was our first-born and when he was just the age you are now, he was stolen by the wizard, Meejeedayjick, and we have never seen him since."

"Meejeedayjick shall pay for this!" cried Kespak. "I shall avenge my brother's death!"

"Yes," said his father, "it is right that you should." But his mother wept, saying, "Now I shall lose my last son!"

Kespak set off that same day with his quiver on his shoulder, his spirit burning with vengeance, hardly able to wait for the moment when he would send an arrow into the wizard's throat. Unfortunately, the wizard was nowhere about, and of all the people Kespak asked, not one could tell him where the fellow lived or when he had last been seen. Kespak traveled and traveled—all over the land of the Passamaquoddy, into the Penobscot country, up into the woods of the Malicete and Micmac—but not a whisper could he hear of Meejeedayjick.

As time passed, the desire for vengeance cooled a little. It was difficult to keep on being angry day after day, particularly when there were so many interesting things to see, so many pleasant people to talk to along the way. He almost forgot sometimes why he had started out from home in the first place. One day, as he was walking through the forest, he met an old man wrapped in a tattered blanket—a man so very old he could barely totter along the trail, and so thin he was more like a *skadegamooch* (a ghost) than a man.

"Help me, young man," implored the old fellow. "Give me food. I am dying of hunger."

Kespak had a piece of tallow in his pouch, just enough for himself for the day's journey, but he gladly broke it in half and gave the old man one piece; then seeing how the *skadegamooch* (as Kespak called him in his mind) swallowed it with frantic haste, the boy gave him the other half as well, telling himself he was young and would soon reach a village where food would be offered him in abundance.

He was due for an unpleasant surprise, however. When the old man had eaten, he told Kespak he had just come from the next village and the people there were starving.

"Game has been scarce in this district all winter, and now Spring has come, things are no better. We have lived for months on the few fish we could get from the river. Our hunters have gone in all directions and have found not even the trail of game. They say all the caribou have disappeared, and it is on caribou we chiefly depend."

Kespak began to regret parting with his tallow so quickly.

"You are a strong, active young fellow," said the *skade-gamooch*. "Can't you find where the caribou have gone, and bring them back?"

"If under the spur of hunger your own young men have been unable to find them, how can I, a stranger, manage it?" asked Kespak.

The old man put his finger to the side of his nose and winked. "*I* know where the caribou have gone," he said, "but they won't listen to me."

Kespak began to wonder if the old man was mad. He said hurriedly "I'd like to help you, but as a matter of fact I can't really afford the time. I am on an important mission. I have promised to find the wizard Meejeedayjick and pay him back for the murder of my brother."

"Vengeance will not bring back the dead," said the old man, "but caribou will feed the living."

33

"I cannot dishonor my parents," said Kespak, "by letting that wizard go unpunished!"

"Your parents would be better off with a son to care for them in their old age," said the *skadegamooch*. He gave the boy a sly look as he added, "However, if you must find Meejeedayjick, I can tell you where he is."

"You can?"

"But only after you have found the caribou."

Kespak hesitated. Was it foolish even to listen to this old man? Yet here at last was possible information as to the wizard's whereabouts. It might be a wild goose chase, yet if he refused, the *skadegamooch* would think his story made up to get out of helping him—or even think Kespak a coward! This decided the boy.

"Tell me where the caribou have gone," he said, "and I'll try to get them back."

"Well done!"

The old man pointed to a large cloud drifting lazily above a distant hill. "Go in a straight line to that cloud and walk under it. If you are quick, you will reach the other side before it falls. The one who has stolen the caribou uses the cloud as a gate, not only to keep the caribou in, but visitors out. Will you risk it?"

"Certainly," said Kespak. "I am not afraid of the cloud-gate, but it's ridiculous to tell me to go in a straight line. Whoever walked through the forest in a straight line?"

"You will!" The old *skadegamooch* chuckled and fumbled under his blanket. Suddenly all the trees and rocks between Kespak and the cloud toppled sideways, leaving a Path that Led Straight to the cloud.

This old man, thought Kespak, is not so feeble as he looks!

"You will wait here for me?" Kespak was careful to ask. "You have promised to tell me where I can find Mee-jeedayjick, remember."

"I promise to meet you outside the gate. And if you still want to know where to find him, I will tell you."

So Kespak started off and in a little while arrived at the end of the Path that Led Straight. There was the cloud, pink in the dying sun, directly overhead. Kespak started his dash. As he ran, the cloud began to fall—slowly at first, then faster. With his heart in his mouth, Kespak flew over the ground and one last leap carried him safely under the descending cloud.

Kespak found himself safe in a great meadow on the far side of which was a large wigwam. All around the meadow browsed hundreds and hundreds of caribou. A man came out of the wigwam and rushed toward him, shouting.

"What are you doing on my property?"

The boy looked at the thin, hungry looking man with the hard eyes and decided it was best not to mention his real errand, so he pretended to be an ordinary traveler.

"I have come a long way. I am hungry." He expected

the man to invite him to a meal, but the fellow only stared at him with suspicious eyes.

"If you want food," he said at last, "you must work for it."

What sort of Indian was this, Kespak asked himself, who had not the pride to show hospitality even if he had to go hungry himself? Only the very worst of people refused food to a stranger.

"Very well," said Kespak scornfully. "What work must I do?"

"Guard the caribou. See that none escape. I have gathered this herd with great labor, for I must have food."

"No one could eat all these in a normal lifetime."

"I can. The more I eat, the thinner I get, and the thinner I get, the more I eat."

"How long must I guard them?"

"As long as I say. And if you try to escape, I shall turn you into a caribou!" The man threw the boy a piece of dried meat and went away.

Kespak sat on a rock while he ate and thought to himself that he had been a great fool to listen to the old *ska-degamooch*. The food, however, restored his spirits and he muttered aloud, "I believe I could get under that cloud again if I ran fast enough."

"Don't try," said a mournful voice. "It's no fun being a caribou, especially one in daily expectation of being eaten."

Kespak looked up and saw a caribou regarding him sadly.

"Did you speak?"

"Yes," said the animal. "I was once a boy like you, brought here to tend the flock. One day I tried to escape and I was turned into—this!"

"The man must be a wizard!" marveled Kespak.

"He is. His name is Meejeedayjick."

"Meejeedayjick!" the boy exclaimed. "At last! That is the enemy I have sworn to kill, in order to avenge my dead brother!"

"What was your brother's name?" asked the caribou, and when Kespak told him, great tears sprang into the creature's eyes. "I am Masu! Now our parents have lost both their sons, for there is no hope of killing that wizard. Spears and arrows simply fly off his body."

"My brother—and still alive!" cried Kespak joyfully. "Why, that old *skadegamooch* must have known all this and sent me here on purpose to find you, as well as the lost caribou. We must escape!"

"Others have tried," said Masu mournfully. "None has succeeded. With his magic moccasins, Meejeedayjick can run faster than any caribou."

"We'll see," said Kespak cheerfully, and put his wits to work. "You don't mind, do you, Masu, if I climb on your back?"

"Not at all."

So Kespak climbed on his brother's back and began to ride about. At once Meejeedayjick came out of his wigwam and shouted, "You will wear the flesh off that caribou."

"From his back, however, I can see over the whole flock and thus guard them better," Kespak called to him.

"See that you do!" And the wizard went back into his lodge.

The new herdsman rode his steed closer and closer to the gate, examining the cloud carefully as he approached it. Kespak saw that it rested firmly on the ground. There was no possibility this time of getting underneath—but what about going through? It didn't look solid. Perhaps its gatelike appearance was simply an illusion. He glanced toward the lodge and saw the wizard watching.

"It's now or never, Masu. Make for the gate and don't let that cloud stand in your way. The rest—" he shouted to the herd. "Follow me!"

Away bounded Masu and all the other caribou followed. Crowding behind, they got in the wizard's way just as Kespak had hoped they would. He heard Meejeedayjick cry, "You can't get through that cloud," but Masu plunged straight into the thick white mist. It was icy cold inside and smelled of snow, yet there was nothing substantial about it at all, and in a moment they were out on the other side. There lay the Path that Led Straight. The rest of the herd came pounding past, stopped short—then, seeing they were free, turned and scattered in all directions.

Kespak looked back and saw that the wizard's way was now clear and he was coming like the wind, his magic moccasins hardly touching the ground. Then suddenly the

old *skadegamooch* rose up in the wizard's path and threw his ragged blanket on Meejeedayjick who turned at once into a caribou and ran off with a snort into the forest.

Kespak dismounted and thanked the old man. Without his tattered blanket, the *skadegamooch* looked not only younger but taller, and when he touched his belt there was magic of another kind. Masu the caribou became Masu the boy. The brothers fell into each other's arms, pounding each other joyfully. A moment later, when they looked around, the stranger was gone. Kespak stared at Masu with sudden wild surmise. "I believe that *skadegamooch* was our Great Chief, Glooscap!" And of course it was.

As the two brothers set off for home together, far off on Blomidon the Master remarked to Marten and Noogumee,

"Revenge promises much but pays little." He blew a great cloud of smoke from his pipe into the sky. "Kindness and courage pay much better."

And there, *kespeadooksit,* the story ends.

Kitpooseagunow

ONE OF THE *kookwes* of Glooscap's time was a giant named Kukwu who was very short-tempered. When in one of his sudden violent rages, he would kick the earth and make it tremble. Then the Wabanaki would shiver and say to each other, "Look out! Kukwu is in a rage again."

Now this giant had in one of his wiser moments married a mortal—a gentle and affectionate woman of the Micmac tribe whom he loved greatly—and while she lived, she managed to keep Kukwu in good temper. She died, however, when their son was born, leaving Kukwu to care for Wasis alone. (Wasis is the Wabanaki word for baby.) Kukwu gave his son no other name, knowing it would be changed anyway when the boy grew up. Indians believe that a person's name has special power in it. It ought to be selected, they say, by the owner himself and not mentioned too often or its power is used up.

Sad at the loss of his wife and aware that he was too violent a man to care for a baby, Kukwu was at his wits' end to know what to do with Wasis. Finally, he hit on what he thought was a good plan. He put the babe on a raft and let it drift down a wide and gentle river, hoping some Indian would find the boy and care for him. Then Kukwu dived into the earth and traveled underground to other parts of the world—and that is why earthquakes seldom trouble the land of Glooscap, although in some parts of the earth Kukwu's rages cause great destruction.

Meanwhile, Wasis floated on his ramshackle craft down the river, staring at the blue sky overhead, waving his tiny fists, and laughing at the breezes that tickled his toes. Soon the water began to move more quicky and the raft to bounce up and down on the waves. The stream became narrower, its banks drawing close together. Then, suddenly, with gathering speed, the raft shot into a tunnel into darkness and was carried along on an underground river. It rocked and pitched on invisible rapids, spun about in a dozen whirlpools, avoiding unseen rocks by a miracle. Then, having passed completely under the Micmac and Malicete countries, it arrived beneath the land of the Penobscots. During this wild ride, Wasis ought to have been flung off any one of a hundred times, yet strangely when his vessel shot out into sunlight again, Wasis was still a passenger and had, moreover, in miraculous fashion, become a boy four feet tall, as well developed in his body and faculties as a twelve-year-old.

Now this was magic, the kind that comes—so the Wabanaki believe—from passing successfully over an underground river. They would have told you that on this journey, Kukwu's child had been born again, and that that was why he forthwith took the name Kitpooseagunow, which means "one born after the mother's death." It is certainly a fact that the boy in some unknown manner grew up conscious of his heritage and his powers. He was the son of an immortal, as well as of a good and loving mother, and he resolved to be worthy of both by spending his days in service to humanity.

"I shall rid the world of all evil giants, sorcerers, and Chenoos," he decided, "all beasts, birds, and booöins who prey on the innocent," and he looked about at once for somewhere to begin, but there was no humanity of any kind in view.

He disembarked therefore and traveled through the land until he came to where a young Penobscot couple had their hunting lodge. In the customary hospitable fashion of Indians, they invited Kitpooseagunow to share their meal. It was a desolate place among rocks and Kukwu's son asked why they lived in such a bleak and unproductive spot. He learned that it was because they wished to be near their only child, a boy stolen recently by a booöin who lived in a cave close by. They saw the boy occasionally in the distance and knew that he was still alive. They hoped that in time the wicked sorcerer would release him and send him home.

"To act is better than to hope," said Kitpooseagunow and he asked the Penobscot to make him a bow of white oak. Mystified, but willing, the man set to work. It was a long and wearisome task splitting the bow stave out of a log, cutting and scraping it to shape with beaver-tooth knives, then greasing it, hanging it to season, and greasing it again—but at last it was done. Kitpooseagunow asked the wife for a single strand of her hair and tied it to his bow. He then showed by drawing back the hair in a sharp tug, which bent the bow double, that this was the strongest bowstring they had ever seen. It was apparent now that Kitpooseagunow was not only strong but something of a magician. The boy himself made arrows from straight branches of the dogwood tree, then carved pointed slate-heads and lashed them to the arrow shafts with sinew.

Thus armed, he went to the booöin's cave and called out to the sorcerer that if he did not return the child to his parents at once, it would be the worse for him. The booöin rushed out in a fury but, taking one look at Kitpoose-agunow, burst out laughing.

"What big talk from a half-grown boy!" he jeered, but he never spoke again, for a slate-tipped arrow pierced his heart and he died. Then Kitpooseagunow took the boy back to his parents, who wept with joy and gratitude.

And Kitpooseagunow was now five feet tall.

He bade the Penobscot couple farewell and went on his way. As he walked through the trees, he came to a small stream and was about to jump across when a giant skunk leaped in front and barred the way. "Stop!" cried Abukchelo. "Pay me a token or I'll show you my tail!" To show his tail is a skunk's warning that he will deliver his "ammunition," for he must always turn himself about first.

"What sort of token?" asked Kukwu's son.

The skunk stamped his feet in a stiff-legged dance as a warning of what at any moment he might do.

"Give me two big boys like yourself for my dinner!"

Kitpooseagunow wasted no time in idle talk but, fitting an arrow to his bow, sent it straight to the heart of the black and white bully, who died where he stood. Then Kukwu's son hung the body over a branch of a tree.

"Now show your tail there," said Kitpooseagunow.

He was now six feet tall.

He said to himself with pride, "I have killed a wicked booöin and an evil beast, already. It is clear that I am destined for great things."

He went on his way, alert for new opportunities, and came next day to a village where the people lived in terror of a Chenoo. A Chenoo is a cannibal who once was a human being. Through doing evil, he has grown devilish and likes to feed on human hearts. His habit before setting

45

out to find a victim is to coat himself all over in sticky balsam, then roll in small sticks and stone, and thus he presents a fearsome spectacle to all who see him. He makes a
terrible whoop as he rushes to battle, a sound so awful it
can deafen or even kill one who does not know enough to
stuff moss in his ears.

"It is useless," said the people despairingly, "to deny him
his meal. If we try to stop him, he will kill us all."

"We shall see," said Kitpooseagunow.

Soon the Chenoo came bounding toward the village.

"Who is my dinner for today?" he howled.

"Today you must go hungry," said Kitpooseagunow,
loosing arrows one by one. The Chenoo jumped as each
one struck him and looked surprised.

"What's this? I've got a pain in my side. And something
is tickling my throat. How itchy my chest has grown!"
He turned himself about in a sickly fashion and started
away. "I don't believe I feel hungry today after all. Perhaps
I had better go back to my cave and rest." But long before
he got to his cave, the Chenoo was dead, and there was no
weeping for him among the people of the village or anywhere else.

All the people shouted with joy and offered gifts to
Kitpooseagunow. He accepted in a grand manner and
puffed out his chest, feeling sure that no creature on earth
could ever stand against him.

He was now eight feet tall.

"I am indeed a great man," he told himself, "probably the greatest in the land." And he went on his way, eager for more triumphs.

As the day advanced, Kitpooseagunow grew thirsty, but could find no water. There was the bed of what had once been a lake, yet not a trickle remained in it. All the streams were dried up and there were no springs. Dry of tongue and throat, Kukwu's son came at last to a lodge in the middle of an arid plain and saw people going in and out of it in great numbers. It took him a moment to see that although both men and women went in, only men came out and each carried with care a small birchbark cup. What could this strange procedure indicate?

Kitpooseagunow entered with the rest and saw an ugly old witch sitting in the man's place in the wigwam. Many women were busy at tasks about the lodge—cleaning, cooking, making pots, skinning animals. When they wearied, the witch would snatch up a willow rod from the pile beside her and whip the women to work again. Then she would turn to the men standing patiently at the door, each with a woman beside him.

"You want water? Very well, you know what you have to do." Then the men said a sad good-bye to their women-folk, who went to join the other women working for the witch. All about the lodge were huge bark vessels full of water. The women were allowed to drink when they liked, but no man was allowed to dip out a meager cupful of water until he had first paid by delivering a wife or a daughter to the witch. What they were to do when the women were all gone, no one dared wonder.

"Who are you?" the witch snapped at Kitpooseagunow. "I see you are alone. Without payment, there is no water."

"But I see plenty of water," said the young giant, "enough for all, and some to spare." And he tipped over the birchbark vessels one after the other and all the water ran out of the wigwam and went to the lakes, the ponds, the rivers, and brooks where it belonged.

The old witch danced with fury, but she danced even harder when Kitpooseagunow began to whip her with her own willow rods. Maddened by the pain, she turned herself into a tree, and to this day you will see the stripes and tears of her whipping on the bark of all her birch-tree descendants.

Now Kitpooseagunow was twelve feet tall and a full-grown giant.

When the people praised him for saving them from the witch, he nodded smugly.

"Yes, I am certainly the most powerful giant alive."

At this the people looked at each other and, at last, one braver than the rest said, "There is one more powerful, and that is our Great Chief Glooscap."

"And who is Glooscap?" demanded Kukwu's son with a scowl. Having lived such a short life, Kitpooseagunow had never heard of the Great Chief. When they told him

Glooscap was twelve feet tall and a powerful magician besides, Kitpooseagunow burned with a desire to test himself against this new giant. His pride and ambition had grown as fast as his body and he was no longer simply concerned to save the innocent from evil beings, but to prove to everyone the greatness of Kitpooseagunow.

Learning that Glooscap lived on Blomidon, Kukwu's son set out to find him. From afar he spied Glooscap, a giant as tall as himself, standing on the summit. Reaching the lodge in a few strides, Kitpooseagunow saw before him a handsome, benevolent looking man who smiled hospitably.

"Come in," said Glooscap. "Come up to the highest place."

When Kitpooseagunow was seated, the Lord of Men and Beasts offered a pipe to his visitor and for a while the two smoked in silence, quietly measuring each other. It occurred to Kukwu's son for the first time that he had no real reason to try to kill this giant. It was simply a test of strength he wanted.

"Men say you are greater than I," he said at last. "Yet I have destroyed the booöin, killed the Great Skunk, slain the horrible Chenoo. I have made the Water Witch turn into a tree. Now I wish to measure my power against yours."

"Very well," said Glooscap. "By what means?"

"First a test of magic," said the other, "then a fishing contest. After that we will go hunting."

"Agreed." And Glooscap led Kitpooseagunow down to shore. "Can you make a boat for our fishing?"

"Certainly." Kitpooseagunow lifted a stone and cried as he cast it into the water, "By the power of my immortal father, thou art a canoe!" And a canoe danced on the waves.

"Well done," said the Master, "but a canoe is of little use by itself," and taking two twigs, he turned them into paddles.

So, as far as magic was concerned, they were even.

"Now we will go fishing," said Kukwu's son. "Let us see who can first catch a whale."

Since whales are the very largest creatures on land or sea, it was necessary to enlarge greatly their fishing craft and then make themselves at least seven times their ordinary size, and strong in proportion, with spears also in proportion. Then they went out on the sea and fished.

Suddenly Kitpooseagunow threw his spear down into the water like a thunderbolt. As the handle rose again, he snatched it and there on the other end was a good-sized whale. Triumphant, he whirled it around his head and Glooscap smiled.

"You are the winner here," he said. "Now let us go hunting."

Though they hunted all day, Kukwu's son got nothing and Glooscap only one small beaver.

"That is hardly worth eating," said Kukwu's son scornfully. "We must try again tomorrow."

"Not so," said Glooscap with a twinkle in his eye. "The things of tomorrow are for tomorrow. The beaver was caught today." So they skinned the beaver and shared the meat, and truly it was a small meal for such giants.

Then Glooscap gave the skin to his rival to carry and Kitpooseagunow fastened it to his wrist where it was no great weight as they walked through the forest back to Blomidon. As they walked, however, the skin grew larger and larger and larger, until it broke away altogether from the giant's wrist and he had to fasten it to his waist by means of a sapling. Even so, the skin kept growing until, trailing behind, it tore down bushes and trees, leaving a clean path behind them. Then Kitpooseagunow, seeing Glooscap had played a merry trick on him, had to laugh.

"It is as clear as the moon in its first quarter," he admitted frankly, "that you are the better hunter. So far we are evenly matched, it seems. Now let us go back to our usual stature, for great size will not be necessary in our next encounter." Then he laughed. "I think we will have a cold night tonight," he said, and gave Glooscap a look full of meaning. Then Glooscap—who knows all things— knew what was in the young giant's mind. Kitpooseagunow would try to conjure up cold enough to freeze Glooscap before morning.

As the sun went down, Glooscap sent Marten to gather all the fuel he could find and bade him open the great clay pots of oil. This oil he multiplied by magic and then he sat down with Kukwu's son in the wigwam and began to tell stories.

So they sat there all night while Marten and Noogumee huddled in the back of the lodge trying in vain to keep warm. At midnight the oil was gone and there was no fire left. Marten and the housekeeper were frozen stiff, rigid in a coating of ice, but Glooscap and his guest never so much as shivered. The rocks outdoors could be heard splitting and cracking with the cold, but the son of Kukwu and the Great Chief of the Wabanaki talked on, laughing and telling stories until dawn. As the sun rose, sending its warm shafts down on the earth, Kitpooseagunow claimed they were still even.

"You have resisted the cold, but I have killed your friends."

"But tell me," said Glooscap, "can you bring them to life again?"

"I can try," said Kitpooseagunow. *"Numchahse!"* he cried, which is to say "Rise up!" but neither of the frozen people stirred. Then Glooscap spoke.

"Marten, Noogumee. You are overdoing this business of sleeping. Get up and get breakfast."

And instantly from both the ice melted like a frozen river struck by the spear of the sun, and they stood forth alive and well.

"You are the greater," said Kitpooseagunow sadly. "I am not so wonderful as I thought."

53

Glooscap looked at the younger giant with affection.

"But we are so nearly equal as makes no difference," he said, "so let us be friends."

"With all my heart," said Kitpooseagunow.

And so—*keaspeadooksit*.

Wasek and the
Red Giants

GLOOSCAP, the Wabanaki tell us, always kept a large fire
going in front of his wigwam. When the ashes accumu-
lated, he would fling them red hot into the Bay of Fundy
and this caused a vapor to rise, making the famous Fundy
fog—a fog so thick one could hardly see beyond one's
nose. All objects became magnified and distorted—every
floating twig a canoe, every cluster of rocks a group of
mountainous islands, every wave a giant—and that is how
it seemed one day to the Boy Who Always Looked Down.

The boy's real name was Wasek and he was a Micmac
who lived in the very shadow of Blomidon, the home of
Glooscap. Wasek was always wishing for *keskamzit* (magic
power) which, so the Indians believed, could often be
found in stones shaped like birds or animals, and that is

55

why he was called the Boy Who Always Looked Down. He was always looking down at the ground hoping to find a *keskamzit* stone. He thought if he could find one, he wouldn't have to spend a lot of time learning how to handle a fish spear or shoot with bow and arrow—he could get all the meat he wanted by magic, have his weir always full of fish, and become Chief of the tribe one day, respected and feared by all. His parents tried to tell him that *keskamzit* stones were hard to find and it was better for a boy to learn how to do things for himself, in case he never found any —but Wasek wouldn't listen. It was simpler to dawdle on the beach searching for stones than to learn how to make arrows and hunt game.

One day, to escape work, he took the family canoe and paddled out into the bay. When he was a good way out, he laid the paddle down and, stretching out in the bottom of the craft, soon fell asleep.

While he slept, Glooscap threw out his ashes.

The boy woke, chilled to the bone, fog all around him, the shore lost to view. Even the bow of his canoe looked distant and strangely out of shape. Wasek grabbed his paddle anxiously and wondered which way to head. All directions looked alike. If he paddled too far the wrong way, he might find himself in the open sea. As he hesitated, he heard the distant sound of paddles and voices. Eagerly he paddled in that direction. It must be his parents or friends coming to look for him.

"Here I am!" he shouted.

The sounds grew louder and closer, and Wasek laid his paddle down. No use exerting himself. They would find him if he just kept calling. So at intervals he shouted, "Here I am. This way," then calmly waited for his rescuers to appear.

It was strange, however—although the sound of paddles and voices increased enormously, nothing came in view. The sound grew louder still and began to vibrate all around him in a disturbing way. Was this some strange effect of the fog? Wasek seemed now to hear enormous thrashing paddles, the roar of a thousand voices all echoing and groaning in the mist around him! His heart began to beat unevenly and in sudden panic he snatched up his paddle and began to back water, but it was too late. Out of the fog loomed a tremendous canoe paddled by two giants. Catching sight of Wasek, one shouted in a voice that hurt the Micmac boy's ears, "Look! What is that queer looking chip?"

"Let us examine it more closely," said the other, and he put his huge paddle right under Wasek's canoe and lifted it. The Boy Who Always Looked Down felt himself soar upwards, then drop in heart-sinking fashion into the giant's hand. The canoe toppled over, Wasek tumbled out, somersaulting down a slope of dark red skin. A great thumb and forefinger closed over him gently—only bruising him in a dozen places—and set him upright. A voice—so subdued it could only be heard for fifty miles—asked with interest, "My brother, what have we here?"

"A small human," chuckled the second giant and he sounded like Wokwotoonok the North Wind roaring through the forest during an Autumn gale. "I wonder if he's good to eat."

"No, no!" screamed Wasek, thinking his hour had come. "Put me back, I'm much too small!"

The giant bent an enormous ear down to the tiny sound. "What's that? Speak up, little brother."

"I'd hardly make a mouthful," Wasek bawled, and the giant laughed so hard the whole world seemed to shake.

"True enough! Well, we'll take him back with us—a poor catch for a day's fishing!" The despairing Wasek was set back in his canoe, which was then lodged in the crevice under the larger canoe's thwarts. Then the giants turned the bow toward home.

Now these giants belonged to a tribe whose Chief was called Oscoon the Red, and they lived well to the north of the Wabanaki in a country called Akilinek. Ordinarily, a canoe trip from the Bay of Fundy to Akilinek would take a full week, but with these great men paddling, they arrived off the shores of Oscoon's land by nightfall of the same day. The Chief, head and shoulders taller than any of his people, came down to the beach to greet them.

"Ho, my sons!" he roared when he saw Wasek. "Where did you find that little creature?"

"Lost in the Fundy fog, Oscoon. He's a present for you."

"Good!" thundered the Chief. "Bring him to my lodge. He will make a fine plaything for my children."

A plaything for children! Wasek, the Boy Who Always Looked Down, felt his face burn with shame. A miserable end for one who had hoped to be a Chief! He clutched the sides of the canoe as he was carried up to the Chief's lodge. There Oscoon laid him, still in his canoe, in the eaves of the wigwam within easy reach—only about a hundred yards from the ground. A meal was brought by Oscoon's wife, and seeing Wasek was so small, she gave him what she herself would eat as a snack before dinner— not more than enough for six men with ordinary appetites. "Eat!" shouted the woman-giant in a friendly way. "Don't stint yourself. Game's been on the small side lately, but there's plenty of it." She pointed to a hunter bringing in two or three dozen large caribou strung to his belt. "You see? Small things!" Another man came into camp swinging three moose in his hand as a Micmac might swing rabbits, while another strode from the woods with a bear tossed over his shoulder.

Wasek was too sad and miserable to eat more than a few mouthfuls. After the meal, Oscoon's wife gave in to the pleading of the children—not one of whom was under six feet tall—and gave them Wasek and the canoe to play with.

So began Wasek's life with the Red Giants. Though the children meant to be kind, they made the boy's life a nightmare. Bruised and battered even by the gentlest hands, deafened by the softest voice, Wasek was continually nervous and always homesick. He no longer looked down, though. He *had* to look up, in order to see the faces of these people and try to read their expressions, for on their lightest whim his very life depended.

Because he was so small and unlike themselves, the giant-children thought he had no feelings, and because of his weakness they soon considered him poor sport and lost interest in him. Sometimes Wasek was left on the shelf for days at a time, and somehow this was the worst thing of all, to know that he was so unimportant, so useless, that even the children were indifferent to him.

Once or twice he thought of trying to perform for the children—entertain them in some way—make them take notice of him! But what was there he could do? The children had made him a tiny bow and arrow, but he could never manage to hit anything. They gave him a miniature spear, but he failed to catch even one fish. They gave him an animal to skin and he spoiled it. He didn't know how to do these things! He didn't know how to do anything!

One day, the children left him out on the beach all night. In the morning it was raining and the unhappy boy sat, shivering, on a rock, wishing he would die of exposure and so end all his troubles.

A white loon circled overhead, giving its weird unearthly cry, and for a moment Wasek felt a stir of hope. Glooscap, he had heard, often visited his people in the form of a loon. Perhaps he had come to rescue him! "Help me!" he shouted, and he seemed to hear the reply drift back—"Help yourself!"

Shocked, Wasek watched the white loon's swift flight away from the beach. Had those really been the words? Help himself? How could he help himself, small as he was, lost among these huge and powerful people? If he had been given some *keskamzit* now, he might have had a chance! What with the cold and the rain and the disappointment, Wasek began to cry.

Then, quite suddenly, he was angry. Very well! If nobody would help him—if nobody, not even Glooscap, cared enough to stretch out a hand to him—he *would* help himself. He would become strong enough, somehow, to get the best of these giants, and he would begin right now. Wasek flexed the feeble muscles of his arm and flexed them again, this time with more firmness. He bent his knees and straightened them, not once but fifty times. When he was tired, he rested for a while, then started lifting stones—first a small one, then a larger one, and so on. He looked, *not* down at the stones, but *up* with his chin firmly set. One thing and one thing only was on his mind—to become strong!

Day after day, week after week, month after month, Wasek practiced. The children forgot him, the women paid him no heed, the giants were too busy making war with a neighboring tribe to have any thought for such a small piece of humanity. Wasek ate the scraps that dropped from the giants' food dishes and went back to his exercise. He grew stronger and stronger. Very soon he could lift Oscoon's great paddle and hold it over his head.

At last, one day, he went up to one of the children— a four-year old boy who was only about eight feet tall— and shouted, "I could hold you on my hand if I wanted to!"

"Try it!"

Wasek laid his hand flat on the ground and the boy stepped on it, overlapping it on every side, but—slowly— Wasek lifted him until he could hold his hand out on a level with his shoulder. The boy-giant looked down at Wasek in amazement.

"What has happened to you?"

"I am no longer your plaything," said Wasek in triumph, and he set the boy down on the ground. "I am going home now, back to my own people."

He walked quietly into the wigwam and while Oscoon's wife watched, surprised, he climbed up the center support of the lodge to where he could reach his canoe and lifted it down without effort. She simply stared as he carried it out of the lodge and down to the beach, the children trooping after him, wide-eyed.

"Good-bye," said Wasek calmly, and pushed off from shore with his paddle.

"Good-bye!" the children roared, and Wasek covered

his ears for the last time. A white loon soared down from the sky and the boy heard through the loon's mournful cry the words—"Well done, Wasek! Now follow me!" And the Master led him safely home. Glooscap had helped him after all—after he had shown he could help himself.

And so—*kespeadooksit*—the story ends.

The Year Summer
Was Stolen

THE WABANAKI always remember the year Summer was stolen. It was all, of course, the fault of Badger!

Long ago in the Old Time, the Micmac Kekwajoo was considered the most troublesome Indian in all the land. It was said of him that he must have had Lox the Indian Devil for a father. There was certainly a good deal of the Devil in him and since Lox often took the form of a badger in going about the world, Kekwajoo came to be known as Badger, the Mischief Maker.

Badger lived mostly in the Micmac country, traveling about a good deal with his small brother. Both lived mostly on the labor of others and spent the rest of their time amusing themselves. One winter, however, Little Brother fell ill. Badger who, to do him justice, was truly devoted to the boy (though he cared not a choke-berry for any other person in the world) nursed his brother with great tenderness and saw him through the worst of the sickness. As the winter dragged on, however, Little Brother still lay all day looking wan, refusing food. Badger coaxed him to try all the tidbits he had begged or stolen for him, but it was no use. The boy just sighed and said weakly, "I shall be all right when Summer comes." Which was all very well, but Summer was still three or four months away and Little Brother might die in the meantime.

So it was that Badger decided to steal Summer from her home in the South and bring her to the Wabanaki land ahead of time. Now Badger knew, as did everyone, that Glooscap had given Winter, the Ice King, the right to spend six months of every year in the land of the Wabanaki. Then he had to move to the far North, leaving the other six months to Summer. That was the rule, but little cared Badger for rules! He had made up his mind and that was that.

He knew it would not be easy. Summer lived south of the Passamaquoddy in a large airy wigwam on a lake. The wigwam was carefully guarded by strong braves, two by day and two by night. To Badger, however, the risk simply added to the fun.

Leaving Little Brother to the care of a kindly neighbor, he set off in his canoe to find and capture Summer. On the first day of his journey he met Keewasu the muskrat.

"Keewasu," said Badger, "if you will help me bring Summer to the Wabanaki land, I shall give you on our return a hundred cattails." This was the muskrat's favorite food and the wrong time of year for them to be growing, so naturally he agreed to accompany Badger on the expedition.

On the second day, they met Madooes the porcupine.

"Madooes," said Badger, "I will give you all the salt you want as soon as you have helped me capture Summer."

The porcupine licked his lips, for there is nothing he likes better than salt, and he hadn't had a lick since last summer. He agreed to go with them.

On the third day, they met Wokwes the fox.

"Wokwes," said Badger, "I know you are fond of rabbits. I promise that if you help me bring Summer to the Wabanaki before the next full moon, you will have all the rabbit dinners you can eat."

"How delicious!" said the fox, and joined them at once.

As they traveled on, the air grew warmer and was filled with sunlight and the fragrance of flowers. Finally they came to a large lake dotted with water lilies. On the shore of this lake stood Summer's lodge. Badger sent his three scouts to spy out the land.

Creeping close, the animals saw Summer swimming in the lake. Presently she came out of the water and went into the wigwam and the door-flap closed. The braves took up their positions outside, spears in hand, and the animals went back to report to Badger.

"She's there all right," said Wokwes.

"We'll never get her away though," said Madooes.

"Those guards are too much for us," said Keewasu.

"Here's what we'll do," said the indomitable Badger, and he whispered his plan.

That night, shortly after moonrise, the muskrat slipped into the water on the far side of the lake and began to make a noise like moose pulling up water lilies—a sort of "swish-crunch" kind of noise—while the porcupine was busy eating holes in the guards' canoe and nibbling the paddles halfway through. At a signal from Badger, the fox began to bark with all his might.

"What's that!" cried the guards, hearing as they thought the sound of moose feeding. Then, as the fox began to bark —"That fox is excited! Game must be close. Perhaps Team has come to feed on the water lilies!" Forgetting everything except the wonderful taste of good venison, they rushed to the canoe and shoved it into the water. When they were halfway across the lake, the paddles broke and the canoe began to fill, and the next thing they knew they were floundering in the water. Meanwhile Badger was at the wigwam door.

"Summer! I've come to take you to the land of the Wabanaki."

"But it's much too early," said the surprised Summer.

"You must come all the same," said Badger firmly, "or my brother will die!"

Now Summer was soft-hearted and soon let Badger persuade her, thinking she could make just a short visit and then return. So she ran with Badger to his canoe and they set off for the North. Wokwes, Madooes, and Keewasu rushed to the lake's edge, calling to Badger to wait for them, but the impatient Mischief Maker paid no heed. The three were left stranded on shore.

The moment Badger arrived with Summer in the land of the Wabanaki, the ice began to melt, the snow to run in the brooks, and the buds to burst on the trees. Badger hurried Summer to his lodge and Little Brother, seeing her, sat up and smiled. "Stay with me," he begged. So Summer stayed.

Soon everything in the country was topsy-turvey!

The skunk cabbage came rushing up through the earth expecting to find herself in a snowbank. Instead, the land was brown, with green shoots popping everywhere—and she was furious to think that other plants had got ahead of her. The flies, smelling the skunk cabbage, started to scrabble their way out of the trees. The raccoons, smelling *them,* scampered up the trees to investigate. Moonumkweck the woodchuck, or groundhog, emerged from his burrow rubbing his eyes, surprised that it was time to get up. Mooin the bear, waking as he often did to go for a short walk on the snow, felt his feet sink in pools of water and was outraged. Mooin hated getting his feet wet. Bats woke and flew around in a daze. A butterfly struggled out of its cocoon before it really wanted to, and Ableegumooch the rabbit was alarmed to find himself in a brown and green world still wearing his white winter coat. What if Wokwes the fox happened by? Does, bucks, and fawns who had congregated all winter in places where food and shelter were available suddenly went their separate ways, while Team the moose hurried down from the high country, afraid all the water lilies in the lakes would be gone before he got there. Some creatures made themselves ill on unexpected feasts of buds and insects, while others looked frantically for mates, wondering why they had overslept. Lusifee the wildcat yowled, the red fox yipped, and the rabbit thumped his hind feet. Summer had come too soon. Spring hadn't come at all. The whole Wabanaki world was upside down.

Returning from a hunting trip in the North, the Great Chief Glooscap heard the news and strode down from Blomidon. The land was hot and wet and everyone was rushing about in a frenzy. Knowing at once who was to blame, Glooscap went straight to Badger's wigwam and there, sure enough, he found Summer feeding Little Brother his supper.

Seeing the Master, Badger jumped up with an impudent grin.

"I had to bring Summer ahead of time," he said without the least shame in the world. "Little Brother needed her. As soon as he is well, I shall take her back."

"You will take her south at once!" thundered Glooscap. "And I shall want a word with you, Badger, when you return. As for you, Little Brother, stop being lazy and get up."

Glooscap's word was law. Up got Little Brother and off went Badger to take Summer home.

The sun slipped behind a cloud and the cold breath of the Ice King blew down Badger's neck as he paddled off from shore. When the canoe with Summer in it was quite out of sight, pools and lakes and brooks skimmed over with ice and it began to snow.

The animals stopped their howling and yipping and thumping and looked around in amazement at the changed landscape. The moose sheepishly climbed back up the hill. The deer began looking about for their husbands, rounding up fawns that had gone astray, while the rabbit relaxed, knowing he was at present as safe as he'd ever be from predators like Wokwes. Mooin shook his big feet to dry them and crept back to his den where his wife woke up and complained of his cold feet. Moonumkweck found he had not after all made a mistake and went to sleep again, while the flies burrowed back into the bark and the skunk cabbage sank into the ground to wait for a warmer day. Winter was back. All was normal once more.

Meanwhile Badger delivered Summer safely to her home. When he returned to go down to his canoe, however, he was confronted by three scowling animals.

"Where are my cattails?" growled the muskrat.

"Cattails don't grow in winter," said Badger, not liking the look of Keewasu's sharp teeth. "There would have been plenty if Glooscap had let Summer stay."

"Where is my salt?" demanded the porcupine.

"There would have been all you wanted," grinned Badger, edging away from Madooes' sharp quills, "if the

summer sun had had time to evaporate it from the ocean!"

"And what about the rabbits you promised me?" howled the fox.

"If you'd been there, Wokwes, you'd have seen plenty about," said Badger. "It wasn't my fault that Glooscap chose to bring the snow back."

This was too much for the three and with one accord they jumped at Badger and pushed him into the lake. Then they threw rocks at his canoe and broke it.

"Now get home the best way you can!" they shouted.

"You won't move fast on promises!" And off they went, three sadder and wiser woodland creatures.

"Oh well," said Badger, standing up with the water streaming off him and water lilies in his hair, and thinking of Glooscap's face the last time he had seen it—"I'm in no hurry to get back!"

And there—*kespeadooksit*—the story ends.

Tomik and the Magic Mat

ONCE IN THE ancient time of the Wabanaki, there lived a young widow without children. Her name was Welowna. One day, gathering wood in the forest, she found a baby— an infant so small she could slip it inside her mitten. And the wind whispered to her—"Take care of this child, for there is one who would do him harm."

Resolved to take no risks, Welowna moved to a remote part of the forest and built a wigwam there for herself and the child, and now she was happier than she had ever been in her life. She had a child of her own to care for. Having no milk, she made a sort of gruel from the scrapings of rawhide. Tomik, as she named the boy, thrived on it. By snaring and dressing small game, Welowna was able to provide meat as he grew older, and soon Tomik was able to run and play. When he was four, he asked for a bow and arrow.

"Very well," she said, and she made him a bow six inches long with arrows to fit, and Tomik went on his first hunt in the long grass near the lodge. Seeing a mouse, he shot and killed it and toddled home with all the pride of a mighty hunter.

"I have killed a wild beast," he said with dignity. "Take your carrying strap and fetch home the meat." This was the custom among the Indians, to send a woman to bring back the hunter's kill. Smiling, Welowna went to the grass as instructed and, finding the tiny beast, laid it on her shoulder and carried it home, where she made the hide into a mat for Tomik to sit on.

Another day he announced to her that he had killed a second great beast in the alder bushes by the river near the wigwam. Welowna, receiving his directions, went to get it and this time found a small ground squirrel. She brought it home, skinned it and made another mat, which Tomik gave back to her for her own use. Next he shot a rabbit in a nearby wood, and this was treated in the same manner, and the hide transformed into a mat for any visitor who should chance to come.

After that, Tomik hunted regularly both with spear and bow, and traveled farther and farther from home in search of game. Soon after his twelfth birthday, he saw a giant walking ahead of him through the trees. Now Tomik had never seen a man, much less a giant, yet he knew this was a *kookwes* because Welowna had told him giants were twice as tall as ordinary adults. "There are good *kookwes* like Glooscap and Kitpooseagunow, and bad ones like Winpe and Kukwu and Kaktoogo. One can only know their natures by their acts." So the boy quietly followed the giant, hoping to tell by his actions if he were good or evil.

He saw that as the *kookwes* walked through the forest the birds sang with joy and one flew to perch on his shoulder. Small animals ran and talked to him, and the flowers at his feet nodded welcome. This giant must be good! If he were not, the flowers would be still, the animals would run away, and the birds would hide under the leaves. So he stepped forth bravely and saluted the stranger.

"Kwah-ee, *kookwes!* My lodge is close by. Come and share my evening meal."

The giant accepted with thanks, pleased by the boy's spirit, and they walked along together. As they entered the lodge, Welowna looked up, alarmed at first. Then recognizing the magic belt and the necklace of amethysts, she whispered, with awe—"Glooscap!"

"Come up to the highest place," said Tomik, proud to entertain such a visitor.

Over the evening meal, Glooscap talked to the boy of the outside world and the great affairs going on there, and told stories of Ableegumooch and Kekwajoo, and others who were only names to Tomik. The boy began to yearn for experience of this wider world himself, and when Glooscap left next day Tomik grieved in his heart. No longer was Welowna all his world, as much as he loved her.

"When may I go out to mix with men?" he asked his foster mother.

"When you yourself are a man, Tomik," she answered gently, "strong enough to support and defend yourself." Then she sighed. "If only my husband had lived, you would have had a father to teach you all the things a Wabanaki brave should know."

"Why haven't I a father of my own?" asked the boy. "Where is my father?" It was a question he had never thought to ask before seeing Glooscap.

Then Welowna told him for the first time how she had found him in the woods alone, abandoned, threatened by some unknown enemy.

"As soon as I am a man," said Tomik with determination, "I shall go to look for my father, and no enemy will dare stop me! I shall become strong in the meantime." And from that time Tomik practiced every day with bow and arrow, ran from noon to dark to become fleet of foot, hardened himself to heat and cold and rain, and made his morning bow to the Sun so that his arm would be strengthened when he met his enemy.

On his sixteenth birthday, Tomik shot his first moose. Now at last he was a man! He sped home to tell Welowna but, arriving there, he found the place strangely quiet.

There was no pot on the fire, no cheerful sounds of meal preparation. The fire itself was almost dead. He rushed into the wigwam. There was no one there.

Then a voice spoke from the visitor's place in the back of the lodge. "Your enemy, the Culloo, has been here and taken Welowna away." The voice came from the rabbit skin on which Glooscap had sat. Unknown to Tomik or his foster mother, Glooscap had given the mat voice and sense—*keskamzit* as the Indians call it, or magic power. The boy was too troubled at the moment to marvel, but asked anxiously,

"What is a Culloo? Where has the Culloo taken her? Let me know where the trail begins and I shall follow it to the ends of the earth!"

"The Culloo is a giant bird who lives in a nest at the end of the sky," said the magic mat, "and feeds on humans. You cannot follow him—there are no trails in the sky. However, he told the woman he would come back for you tomorrow. When he comes, you must shout 'Mat, kill' and I shall rise up and destroy him."

So Tomik waited as patiently as he could for the morning when, just as the mat had promised, the bird appeared, darkening the sky with its huge wings. The Culloo glided down with a rush of wind and settled on the ground.

"I see you waited for me. Good. Let us be off."

"Wait," cried Tomik. "What have you done with my foster mother?"

"She is alive and well," answered the Culloo, "though I can't say how long she will remain so. My sons are guarding her. Should I not return, they will kill and eat her at once."

Tomik's lips had just parted to call upon the magic mat to do its work, but hearing that, his lips closed again. If the Culloo died, so would Welowna. If Tomik saved himself, it would be at his foster mother's expense. There was only one thing to do.

"I am ready to go with you," he said, and this was a very brave thing to do, for he had no real hope of saving Welowna, yet he was willing to throw his own life away if necessary in the attempt.

"That's a sensible lad," said the Culloo, and grasping the boy in his great claws, he carried him up into the heavens. In his triumph, he failed to notice that at the last moment Tomik had snatched up the magic mat and made a belt of it around his waist.

The Culloo flew up and up to a great rock at the very end of the sky, and on the rock was a huge nest. There was Welowna surrounded by three fierce young Culloos, and the poor woman wept at the sight of her foster son, thinking now there was no escape for either of them.

There was something Tomik had to know. "Why are you my enemy?" he asked the Culloo. "What have I done to injure you?"

"Nothing," the great bird answered. "I have nothing

against you, Tomik, except the fact that you are your father's son. Capturing and killing you will make my revenge against him complete."

"You know my father?" asked the boy eagerly.

"I know him," said the Culloo grimly, "and my sons know him! He killed my brother. In revenge, I stole his wife and baby. The woman managed to slip the child out of its cradleboard while we were close to the earth. You escaped me then, but I have you now."

Tomik, glancing over the edge of the nest, seeing first the earth very small below, then the giant birds so huge and strong, nearly gave up hope. What use was a small rabbit-skin mat against such creatures as these? Still, he must do what he could.

"Mat, kill!" he cried in a loud voice.

The mat flew from his waist and wound itself like a scarf around the father Culloo's neck. At first the bird laughed and tried to pull the "scarf" away, but it grew tighter and tighter around his throat and finally stopped his breath completely. Tomik took back the mat and the young Culloos flew up in great fright. Two of them managed to escape but Tomik caught the third by his tail feathers and hauled him back into the nest.

"If I spare your life," said the boy, "will you carry my foster mother and me to the village where I was born and where I can perhaps find news of my father?"

"Yes! Anything!"

Taking Welowna by the hand, Tomik helped her mount
the bird's back and climbed up behind her.

"Now take us down," commanded the boy.

Obediently the young Culloo rose, circled the nest, and
shot off into space. Then, feeling safe in his own element,
the air, he cried mockingly, "You have no power over me
now. I can shake you off whenever I please. And if you
kill me with the mat, we will all fall to earth together. You

and the woman will die also. So give me the magic mat and I'll carry you safely."

"Don't trust him," cried Welowna. "Once he has the magic mat, we are helpless."

The boy knew this was true, but what were they to do if the bird threw them off his back? Was there any way the mat could help without also causing their deaths? He decided to take the risk.

"Mat, squeeze!" he shouted, "but not enough to kill!"
The mat leaped from the boy's hand and wrapped itself like a belt about the bird's middle. It squeezed and squeezed until at last the Culloo could stand the pain no longer and howled for mercy. "Stop! I'll take you down if I must, though I'm sure to be killed. Your father has promised to shoot every Culloo on sight."

"So my father is alive!" exclaimed Tomik joyfully.

"He's the Chief of that village below us."

The boy looked down and saw all the people rushing out of the wigwams to stare up at the sky. One, wearing a Chief's feather, began to shoot at them with his bow and arrow.

"Mat—catch!" cried Tomik and the mat caught the arrows in its fibres, thus deflecting them from their target. "Land quickly! You will be safe if you do as I say."

As the Culloo settled on the ground, the Chief came rushing toward them with raised tomahawk.

"No!" cried Tomik. "Let the bird go. He has kept his promise."

"I also made a promise!" the Chief shouted. "Do you know what the Culloos have done to me and my family?"

"I do."

The Chief looked sharply at the boy for the first time and suddenly his eyes glowed with hope. "I see my wife's features before me! Who are you?"

"I am your son," said Tomik.

And so—Tomik and Welowna lived happily thereafter with Tomik's father. The Culloo flew off and the magic mat was put away with care in case Glooscap should ever come to visit again.

And so—*kespeadooksit*.

How Ableegumooch
Tracked a Fox

Long ago when the Wabanaki world was young, Ableegumooch the rabbit appointed himself Glooscap's forest
guide. Whenever he met a Wabanaki who was lost—and
Indians did get lost on occasion—the rabbit was only too
happy to put him on the right path or lead him home.
Ableegumooch enjoyed helping people, so much so indeed
that sometimes he got carried away and ended up doing
more than he intended—like the time he met the Malicete
couple in the forest and discovered that, though they themselves were not lost, they had lost their child.

"I put him down on that mossy knoll," wept the dis-
tracted mother, "while my husband went to cut wood and
I unpacked the food. When I looked around a few minutes
later, my son was gone!"

"Never mind," said the cheerful rabbit, "he cannot have gone far. I shall look for his tracks and see which way he went."

"The babe was in his cradleboard," said the father. This was a padded board to which an infant was bound and then carried on his mother's back.

"Oh!" Taken aback for a moment, Ableegumooch quickly recovered his self-possession. "In that case, he couldn't walk away. He must have been taken away. And whoever took him must have left traces." The rabbit examined the soft ground near the knoll and found distinct foot marks—two pairs obviously made by two different women, and a set of four made by a dog or a fox. The rabbit put his nose to the latter tracks and confirmed his suspicion. "Fox! So here, you see, are the footprints of the guilty parties," he told the Malicetes impressively, "two women and a fox."

"This pair of prints," said the man, "are my wife's. She stood just there when she laid the boy down."

"Just what I was going to point out!" said the rabbit hastily. "The other prints were made by a woman who traveled in company with a fox. Now I have only to follow those tracks to find your child. Wait for me here. I can travel faster alone. Don't wander about, or you will get lost." And off went Ableegumooch on the trail of the child-stealers.

"This is a new experience," the rabbit thought to himself

with a chuckle, "a rabbit tracking a fox! It's generally the other way around!" He would have to be careful when he caught up with those two. Foxes rather fancied rabbits when they were hungry, and they were nearly always hungry! He wondered why a fox and a woman would travel in company, much less combine to steal an Indian child. A fox might just possibly consider eating an infant, but surely no Indian woman would stand by and let him do it!

Now what Ableegumooch did not know was that the fox was a booöin, or wizard, who could take the shape of fox or man as he wished. The woman was his wife, and a witch. The two, having no children of their own, had stolen the Indian baby and were carrying him to their lodge in the Outer World where they intended to pass him off as their own.

"The thing to do first is to track them down," the rabbit told himself. "After that, we will see what must be done."

So he pressed on, following the tracks to the shore of a large lake where he saw a canoe coming across the water. In it was a pretty Indian woman, singing as she paddled. The canoe came to a gliding stop at the rabbit's feet.

"Kwah-ee," said the maiden.

"Hello," said the rabbit. "I'm tracking down a pair of child-stealers. You haven't seen anything of them, I suppose." He described what had happened and showed her the tracks he had followed to the water's edge.

"They must have set off from here by water. See? There is the mark of their canoe in the sand, and there—the prints of a woman's moccasins. And here is where the fox leaped in beside the woman!" Delighted to show off his detective ability, Ableegumooch did not guess for a moment that the maiden who listened so politely was actually the woman he was chasing! The fox had sent his wife back to see if they were being pursued and if so, to delay the pursuer. He, meanwhile, changed into his man's shape, was carrying the child toward the Outer World.

"They have crossed the lake," declared Ableegumooch, then scratched his head with a hind foot. "But in which direction?"

"I may be able to help you," said the witch. "I saw a canoe headed *that* way." She pointed in the opposite direction to that taken by her husband.

"It was those two without a doubt!" exclaimed Ableegumooch. "You see how close I am on their trail? You must excuse me now. I must run around the shore until I find the marks where they have landed, and then—"

"Wait!" said the witch. "There is only one place where they could land, where there are no rocks in the way. I'll take you there in my canoe if you like. Poor babe," she said, pretending to wipe away a tear. "How he must miss his mother!"

"How did you know it was a boy?" asked Ableegumooch in surprise.

89

"I—you mentioned it, I think," she stammered.

"If I did, I don't remember. But never mind that. I accept your offer. I'm not surprised you wish to help in such a deserving cause." And he hopped into the canoe.

When they reached the end of the lake, the rabbit jumped ashore and looked for tracks, but there were none.

"Too bad," said the witch. "Perhaps the canoe struck a rock and upset with all on board."

The rabbit thought for a moment, then shook his head.

"The canoe wouldn't sink. We should see it somewhere about. I'm afraid, you know, that you were mistaken about seeing a canoe at all. It could have been a bird, or a stick on the water. Well, we must go back and start over."

Hastily, the woman thought of another way to divert him. "Teymumkwak, the wild goose who flies over the lake regularly, lives in that meadow beyond the trees. She may have seen the canoe and noticed where it landed. Why not go and ask her. I'll wait for you here."

"Good idea," said Ableegumooch and off he trotted. As soon as his back was turned, the witch transformed herself into a goose and flew ahead of him, landing in the nest just a wing-beat ahead of the rabbit.

"Oh, there you are, Teymumkwak," said Ableegumooch. "Have you seen a canoe carrying a woman, a fox, and a baby?"

"I have," said the goose. "I saw them leave the lake where it empties into a stream. In the rapids farther on, the

canoe capsized. The woman and the fox drowned, but the
baby in its cradleboard fell upon a red lake-herring and
was carried with it down the stream."

Ableegumooch was an optimist.

"If the fish has the cradleboard on its back, then the
child's head may be clear of the water," he said hopefully,
"and may still be alive. If there are rapids, the water is
bound to be shallow. I must follow that herring!"

The witch then told the rabbit where to find the lake's
outlet, feeling safe in the knowledge that it was a long way
from where her husband had promised to wait for her.
Ableegumooch thanked her and headed back to the lake.
The goose, flying overhead, passed him on the way and,
when he reached the canoe, was there in her woman's shape
again.

"I cannot go with you this time," she said. "My canoe
would go aground in that shallow stream."

"That's all right," said Ableegumooch. "You've been a
great help. Now I think I can manage alone." And waving
good-bye, he started around the shore.

When he got to the place where the stream ran down
from the lake, he saw that the banks were impassable by
reason of tangled brush and rocks. The stream, as the
woman had said, was very shallow. He decided, though
unable to swim, he would go by water! Hauling up a piece
of driftwood, he lay across it on his stomach and bravely
launched himself on the fast-running stream, pushing off

with a sturdy hind leg whenever the driftwood caught on an obstruction.

The rabbit sailed rapidly downstream. Presently he was flying through the rapids, holding on with tooth and nail, his heart in his mouth. All went well, however, and gradually the water slowed.

Now he drifted along, peering down through the water for a sight of the herring. The stream twisted and turned in a new direction and went on for a long way without turning again. Suddenly he glimpsed a bit of red beneath his "raft," and a red fish swam lazily into view. On its back was something white. If this was the child, it was surely drowned by now! Then Ableegumooch saw that the white thing trailing along the fish's back was only a piece of sphagnum moss caught in the herring's gills. At that point, in his excitement, Ableegumooch lost his hold and tumbled into the water. It was lucky for the rabbit the water was shallow, or he wouldn't have done any more tracking of foxes that day or any day. As it was, he managed to scramble to shore, dripping wet but alive.

He sat on a rock and thought things over. After all his trouble, he was as far as ever from the criminals he had been following. What to do now? As he sat twitching his whiskers with annoyance, from behind a nearby clump of trees came the wail of a baby.

"Be quiet!" growled a man's voice. "Wife, are you sure no one followed you?"

"I'm sure. There was only the rabbit, and I got rid of him." Amazed, Ableegumooch recognized the voice of the girl who had been so helpful. "He will be a long way from here by now in a different direction. Put the child in the canoe."

Ableegumooch tried to gather his scattered wits. He had found the baby-stealers and one of them he had met before —she had tried to draw him off the scent. Yet he had been able to catch up with them anyway! Then he saw what must have happened—the stream had turned gradually and carried him back in a curve to the meeting place of the fox and the woman.

Suddenly, thinking of the way the girl had fooled him, Ableegumooch was angry. Forgetting the danger, he rushed through the bushes and confronted the two of them. "You wicked witch! Sending me on a wild goose chase! Making me follow red herrings! I know you now! You won't fool me again. And as for you—" He turned to the man. "I don't know where you came from or what you're—" The rabbit stopped with a gulp of dismay. The man had turned into a fox—the biggest one Ableegumooch had ever seen!

The rabbit gave a great backward leap, turned and ran for his life, the fox and the woman after him.

Ableegumooch felt the hot breath of the monstrous fox and thought his time was up. He was too frightened even to think of calling for help from Glooscap!

Far off on Blomidon, however, the Great Chief had been

on the watch and, calling his dogs Day and Night, started to the rescue. Suddenly there he was—between Ableegumooch and his pursuers. The rabbit felt himself lifted high in Glooscap's hand and set down on a huge shoulder, while the fox, seeing he had more than a rabbit to deal with, turned to meet Glooscap's dogs.

"Stop!" shouted Glooscap. "Don't bite!"

At once the dogs rushed at the fox and the more Glooscap shouted "Stop, don't bite," the more they bit and tore, and the more he shouted "Peace," the more they were ready for war. For this was how the Great Chief had trained them in order to confuse and throw an enemy off balance. Soon the dogs had the fox down and the wizard breathed his last. Then Glooscap said gently, "Go at him, bite him," and the animals came to lie at his feet. He petted them for their obedience, and turned to the angry witch.

"Now where is the babe?"

In her rage and disappointment, the witch refused to say. Instead, she cried out, "Would that I could become forever something which would torment all men!" And instantly she was turned into a mosquito and flew away.

"It's all right, Master," Ableegumooch assured Glooscap. "*I* can find the child. I have only to follow the tracks back to where they started chasing me." And that is what he did.

The baby was returned to his happy parents and ever afterwards Ableegumooch called himself by his full title— Glooscap's Forest Guide and Champion Tracker.

Now—*kespeadooksit*—this story ends.

Coolnajoo, the Foolish One

Long ago in the Old Time there lived a boy who, at the death of his parents, was adopted by two cross uncles. They called him Coolnajoo, which means "foolish one," and since no girl would marry either of the bad-tempered uncles, they had no one to keep their lodge and Coolnajoo was left to do the woman's work—the cleaning, the cooking, gathering of wood, and cutting up of game.

Coolnajoo hated the work and did it badly, neglecting the fire and breaking the pottery, and this was not because he was stupid but because his mind was too busy with dreams of some day being a hunter like his uncles.

One day the uncles greased their bowstrings for the hunt, telling Coolnajoo to have supper ready when they got back.

"And do your work properly for once, Foolish One."

When they were gone, Coolnajoo sat down with a sigh, prepared to dream the day away as usual, but the word "foolish" nagged at him. "They call me foolish," he muttered. "I wonder what would happen if I showed them what it really means to be foolish!"

When the uncles returned that night, they found that Coolnajoo had boiled the venison so long it had turned to soup.

"You said to boil it well," he explained.

He had let the trout fall into the fire, where it burned to a crisp.

"You said you liked your fish well roasted!"

He had cleaned the lodge, both inside and out, even to the extent of cleaning out the inside poles, so when the uncles stepped inside, the whole place fell down on them.

"You said to clean it thoroughly!"

Then Coolnajoo fled, knowing tempers would cool in a short time and he could go back.

A few days later, the uncles sent him to a place where they had killed game, telling him to cut it up and bring it home, then salt it down for the "long days," meaning the long days of summer. The boy got the meat, salted it, and carried it to a nearby village where he asked if there was anyone there named Longdays, because if so, he had a supply of meat for him. Very soon, of course, one of the men declared he was Longdays and carried off the meat, chuckling to himself at the boy's foolishness.

97

"I found Longdays and gave the meat to him," Cool-najoo told his uncles that evening.

"You great lump of stupidity," shouted the older uncle. "It was to be salted for our own use next summer!"

"I'm sorry," said Coolnajoo, moving prudently out of reach. "I'll try to do better next time."

Next day they told him to boil the moose bones and skim the fat off the top, which he did. He then went out and spread this fat, which the Wabanaki call tallow, over a large granite rock. When his uncles came home, he told them what he had done. "There's that poor old man lying out there, his back all hard and cracked. I pitied him, so I spread the tallow over him as a salve." When they demanded to see the old man, he showed them the granite rock.

"Beat him!" cried the younger uncle.

"Beating won't put brains in his head," said the elder. "From now on, Coolnajoo, do nothing. We will do the cooking and cleaning ourselves."

"I can go hunting?" asked the boy eagerly.

"You? Certainly not! You are so foolish, you would shoot yourself instead of the caribou. You are good for nothing except, possibly, the running of errands."

Disappointed, Coolnajoo resolved now to seem more foolish than ever.

The next day, the uncles sent Coolnajoo to a lodge on the other side of the lake. "Tell Pitou if he does not send back the canoe he borrowed from us two moons back, we will pay him a visit." (To pay a man a visit means to do him harm.)

So the boy went to Pitou and told him to send back the canoe. "Just put it in the water and direct it toward my uncles' lodge. That is what they said to do." The mystified man did so and of course the canoe simply drifted away and was lost. When Coolnajoo got home and told his uncles what he had done, they were so amazed they forgot to be angry.

"Why did you tell him that?"

"You said he was to *send* back the canoe."

"But someone had to *paddle* it!"

"I never thought of that," said Coolnajoo with a look of surprise. "I'm sorry."

"Kill him!" snarled the younger uncle, but the elder put out a restraining hand. Remembering how tired they both were of cooking and cleaning, he told Coolnajoo to go to the village and find himself a bride.

"Bring her home to take care of our lodge. And remember, don't set her adrift as you did the canoe. Be sure to paddle her home."

"Whatever you say, Uncle."

Picking up a paddle, Coolnajoo walked to the village and asked at the first lodge he came to for a wife. The owner of the wigwam had many daughters and told the boy to take his pick. Coolnajoo chose the nearest and led

99

her down to the shore. "Go into the water," he said. The girl hung back, puzzled. "So I may paddle you home," he explained. "My uncles say that is how it must be done."

The girl ran home and told her father, and soon the angry father appeared. "No child of mine shall have such a fool for a husband! Be off!"

The uncles were astounded at this latest folly. "Truly," they groaned, "you are a greater fool than we thought. That was no way to treat a girl. You ought to have taken her by the hand and walked her home. If she seemed unwilling, you might have given her a kiss or two."

Coolnajoo hung his head and said he would attend to his uncles' instructions more carefully in the future.

"He's hopeless," said the younger uncle, "too stupid to live."

"We will give him one more chance," said the elder. "Coolnajoo, take this beaver skin and trade it for a good hunting dog, and if you come back without it, it will be the worse for you."

The boy took the skin and hurried to the village, where he made a good trade and began to lead the dog into the woods. Bethinking himself of his uncle's instructions, he ordered the dog to stand on its hind legs and walk along beside him holding his hand. When the dog showed no willingness to obey, Coolnajoo clasped the dog affectionately in his arms and kissed it. The dog gave a howl, broke from his grasp, and fled to the village.

When Coolnajoo arrived home without the dog and told his story, it was too much for the uncles.

"It's true!" screamed the elder uncle. "He *is* too foolish to live! Put him in that sack and tie it up!" Bag and boy were rushed to the shore and there buried in sand up to the neck. "Let the tide cure him of his foolishness," he heard his younger uncle say. Their footsteps went away across the sand.

At last Coolnajoo began to regret his foolish tricks. "If they don't get over their rage before high tide, I shall drown," he groaned aloud. Clams, deep in their sand lodges, heard and came up through their breathing holes to see who it was. "Only a bag of bones," said their Chief, and they all went down again. Somewhere Kakakooch the crow shouted hoarsely. Coolnajoo had an inspiration.

"Hush, brother clams," he said loudly, imitating the voice of the Chief, "for there is Kakakooch listening. Be quiet or he will go and tell Wokwes the fox where he can find some clams, packed full of nourishing iodine and minerals."

Wokwes is a careful eater, always anxious to try new kinds of foods, and he is also a famous digger. Kakakooch is of course a great busybody and talebearer, so the boy's plan worked. The crow flew off to tell Wokwes, who came bounding to the shore, teeth all ready to deal with the clams. The first thing he saw was the top of a sack sticking out of the sand.

"What's this?" He began to dig, and when he had got the bag all up, he broke the string with his teeth and Coolnajoo sprang out, giving the fox such a scare he yelped and ran for his life.

"Much obliged to you, Wokwes," laughed Coolnajoo, "and to you, Kakakooch." Then, hearing the voices of his uncles, he dropped a stone in the bag and ran to hide behind a rock. The uncles, in calmer mood now, had come down to the beach to release their nephew.

"He can't help being foolish, I suppose."

"No. We can't punish him for what he can't help."

But when the uncles opened the bag and found it empty except for the stone, it began to dawn on them that perhaps Coolnajoo was not so stupid and helpless as he seemed.

"Here I am," cried the boy, springing out from behind the rock. "Tell me, did you have good hunting? I hope so, for I have been so tied up all day I have had no time to gather eggs or pick berries." This time Coolnajoo had gone too far. The uncles guessed at last that he had been making fun of them and their rage knew no bounds.

"Back in the bag!"

"Wait," the boy pleaded, "I was only joking."

But they tumbled him back in the bag. "The tide will take too long. Carry him up to the cliff and throw him over."

This time, Coolnajoo realized, there would be no time for his uncles' wrath to cool. He was as good as dead. How he wished he had been content to be called a fool without actually being one!

"O thou Foolish Ones!"

The voice came from a distance. It was like a waterfall dropping from a height, like a rushing wind through the pines, like the great ocean pounding on sand—and it startled the uncles so much they dropped the sack and it flew open, releasing the boy.

All three Wabanaki trembled, knowing at once whose voice it was.

"True, O Glooscap!" quavered the younger uncle, "The boy grows more foolish every day."

"He whose lodge is made of bark," thundered the voice, "should not throw stones at another's. Men of good sense do not give way to childish temper. Go home now, all of you, and mend your ways!"

None stayed to argue! The foolish boy and the foolish uncles hurried home as fast as they could, and if they weren't all more sensible after that, they certainly ought to have been!

And so—*kespeadooksit*—the story ends.

The Great
Penobscot Raid

MENAAGAN, the Penobscot captive, walked back to the Mohawk palisade with an armload of firewood, and as she passed the shocks of corn she noticed something lying on the ground. The white and purple pattern stood out sharply against the yellow of bleached grass, and she bent to look at it more closely. Her heart gave a tremendous leap. It was a belt of spruce-root fibers she had woven for her husband, Pulwaugh, long ago when both were happy in their home in the Penobscot country. She recognized both the dye and the pattern.

What was it doing here in the Mohawk land, far from their Penobscot village where Pulwaugh had been struck down? Did this mean that he was alive after all, somewhere close at hand? Had he left the belt in the path to warn her of his presence? It must be! Should she pick it up? No. The Mohawks lounging at the gate might notice. Menaagan walked on, and entered the palisade of wooden stakes.

What did Pulwaugh want her to do? Was he alone or with a war party? Was she to wait in the long house for him to come for her? Surely not. The long house would be crowded with Mohawk families. Then did he want her to come to that place where the belt was after the camp was asleep? Much more likely! It would not be easy to creep away without being seen, but she would try. How they would get away from Mohawk territory, she could not imagine. She must leave that to Pulwaugh.

Menaagan passed through the gate, not hurrying, trying to appear the usual silent and unhappy prisoner. She must wait through the long day and not allow the enemy to suspect that her heart was dancing with hope.

The women of the various families in the long house where she lived seemed to notice nothing, and she managed to do her work as usual. At last the sun slipped down behind the trees and Menaagan seated herself in the doorway of the house with some mending. As the blue of the evening deepened to black, the people came in and prepared for bed. Soon they would all be asleep. Fortunately it was not the custom of the Mohawks to set guards at night, for they had no fear of being surprised in their own strong village. Menaagan would be able to creep away quietly as soon as the moon—

What was that! A sudden uproar at the gate set the dogs to barking.

Menaagan's heart sank like a stone. Six Mohawk warriors entered the palisade with a pair of prisoners—Pulwaugh, her husband, and Nokum, her brother. She sat very still as they passed and Pulwaugh's eyes stared past her, showing no recognition. She knew therefore that she must pretend not to know him. When the Mohawk Chief summoned her, she went with a calm, indifferent face.

"Woman, these men speak a Wabanaki dialect," the Chief said. "You, a Penobscot, may understand them. Ask what they are doing here and if they are alone."

Menaagan put the question quietly and Pulwaugh answered with a taunting smile.

"Four moons past, the Mohawks paid our tribe a visit. We have grown lonely for our friends and have come to return the compliment."

The Mohawks moved uneasily when they heard the translation, for this was the roundabout Indian way of saying the Wabanaki men had come with a war party to seek revenge. Menaagan was told to ask how many braves were in the party and how far off they were encamped, but this the prisoners refused to answer.

"Very well," said the Mohawk Chief, "you have from

the setting of the sun to its rising to choose how you will die. If by morning you answer our questions, you will be given the mercy of a quick death. Otherwise, you will be tortured and die slowly." And he ordered the captives tied to stakes in the center of the palisade.

Menaagan was obliged to follow the others back to the long house without so much as a glance at her husband and brother. Her heart was sore, for their fate was now certain. Their scouts failing to return by morning, the Penobscot war party would assume the enemy was warned, and would not risk an attack. There might not even be a war party! Pulwaugh and her brother might have come alone. The more she thought about it, the more she was sure this was so.

She resumed her place by the door and sewed with trembling fingers. Anything that might be done must be done by her alone. Should she try to set them free? If she succeeded, it would be only a brief respite. They would be overtaken and brought back. Yet something must be attempted before it was too late! Time was passing. Menaagen tried to come to a decision.

A mosquito buzzed loudly in her right ear and she brushed it away. It came again on her other side and buzzed louder than ever, and suddenly she found herself listening with strained attention. It was a voice speaking in her own tongue!

"Menaagan, my daughter," were the words she heard,

"do as I tell you. They may yet be saved." It was the voice of the Great Chief, Glooscap! "Collect all the moccasins and hide them. Tie strings across all the doorways. Then go and cut the prisoners' bonds. Tell them to go outside and stand at the gate making a great noise. At the last moment, go and pour water on all the fires. You under-understand?" Menaagan nodded breathlessly and the mosquito circled, disappeared with a whine into the night.

Menaagan rose with fast-beating heart. It was quiet now except for the light crackle of the campfire and the cry of a night-bird. The people slept. Moving like a shadow, the Penobscot woman crept about gathering up the moccasins of the men. When she had them all, she hid them under a pile of skins. Then she stole about tying strings of rawhide across all the doorways. For good measure, she scattered sharp stones on the ground. A woman stirred in her sleep, murmuring, and Menaagan stood like a rock. A brave turned over with a grunt. Then all was still again.

Menaagan ran to the prisoners and whispered to them what they must do, at the same time cutting the cords that bound them. Arming themselves with sticks from the pile of firewood, Pulwaugh and Nokum slipped out through the gate and waited for the signal. Menaagan was back in the long house now, lifting the heavy bark vessels and pouring water on the fires. The flames scattered and went out with a hiss of steam and the woman fled into the darkness.

The Mohawks awoke with muttered cries and felt in

109

vain for their moccasins. The steamy air confused them and they crashed into each other in the dark. Then from outside came the frightening sound of Penobscot war cries. The two young men were each making as much noise as ten, whooping and beating their clubs against the palisade. Now the dogs began to add their barking to the rumpus and the children to cry and the women to scream. It sounded to the Mohawks as though they were being attacked by an entire army.

Feeling in the dark for weapons, they rushed out of the

long house only to trip over the strings and fall headlong. Picking themselves up, they danced as the sharp stones cut their feet, and struck blindly at shapes in the steamy darkness, thinking they struck at the enemy. In their excitement, they confused friend with foe, and soon nearly half the Mohawk braves were stretched on the ground with bleeding heads, every one struck down by a friend. Those who were left started for the gate, but the Penobscots were waiting, their eyes accustomed to the gloom, their clubs ready. As each Mohawk emerged through the narrow gate-

way, the sky seemed to fall on him. One after another, the Mohawks were dispatched in this way until only the three Penobscots stood on their own feet.

"Quickly now—to the river," whispered Pulwaugh, and taking Menaagan's hand he led her to the shore where Nokum drew the canoe out of hiding and launched it. Swiftly in the darkness they crossed the stream. Then the two men bore it to the next stream, Menaagan carrying paddles and blankets, and so on until they reached their own country seven days later.

"But didn't the Mohawks come after you?" asked their friends at home in amazement.

"No," said they, and only Glooscap knew why.

It was some hours before all the Mohawks had picked themselves up from the ground and recovered from ringing headaches, but when they had, they congratulated themselves on their narrow escape. "What a terrible battle," they said. "The enemy must have numbered thousands to attack us like that in our own village! We beat them off, of course, but it was fortunate we were not all killed!" And for years they talked of the Great Penobscot Raid, never knowing that the raiding army had consisted of two men and one brave woman.

And so—*kespeadooksit*—the story ends.

Lox and the
Chief's Wife

LONG AGO in the Old Time, there lived a woman named Sakum, widow of a famous Chief. Her husband was dead and all her children grown and married. Still strong and capable, Sakum lived by herself in the forest, caring for her own needs and asking help of no one.

One day she heard that Nabeskus, an elderly woman in her old village, had become homeless at the death of her only son, and out of kindness and pity, Sakum invited the woman to live with her and share her food. Nabeskus, a mean-natured woman, came hoping to live a life of ease and luxury. Sakum, however, soon saw through her and made her do her share of the work.

The women lived in friendship for some time. Then one night, when they were asleep, they had a visitor. Lox, the

113

Indian Devil, walked the earth in many disguises so he could deceive people and cause trouble among them. This time he came in the shape of a raccoon. Taking a stick from the woodpile, he poked it into the still burning embers of the fire until it was red hot, then applied it to the bare foot of the sleeping Nabeskus. She woke with a scream and, hopping about on one foot, accused the Chief's wife of burning her. This, of course, Sakum denied. Grumbling and complaining, Nabeskus lay down again, and both went to sleep. Lox now played the same trick on Sakum, who jumped up with a cry of pain and surprise. She woke the other woman and wanted to know why Nabeskus had tried to injure her. Nabeskus naturally denied having done so, and soon they were quarreling, nearly coming to blows. At this, the watching Lox was delighted, for war of any sort was the thing he liked best. Seeing the dissension his trick had caused, he laughed and laughed. He laughed so hard, he literally split his sides and died, and so missed seeing the women make their peace at the end. In the morning, they got up and found the dead raccoon at their door.

"Good," said Sakum, seeing the scorched poker lying nearby and guessing what had happened. "We'll have him for dinner."

The women skinned the raccoon, hung the skin on a bush, and put the kettle on the fire. When the water was good and hot, they dropped him in. Now Lox was of course immortal and never remained dead for long, but smoke,

fire, and heat were what he dreaded most. He gave a yell and leaped out of the pot. Rushing off, he grabbed his skin, put it on and vanished. Even in his escape, however, he made more mischief, for he kicked the pot over as he jumped. The hot water spilled on the fire, throwing up hot ashes in the face of Sakum and blinding her.

Now this made things very hard for the Chief's wife. Not only had she to suffer the misery of blindness, she could no longer go hunting or fishing and was dependent on her companion for most of her wants. Nabeskus had no complaints, for Sakum's blindness suited her well. Now she could keep out all the best things for herself. Every day she put a miserable dish of food in front of Sakum, saying,

"The meat is poor today, but it must do. You may be sure, however, that I have given you the best, since you are blind."

Sakum did not suspect that the woman was deceiving her, and thanked her warmly. So Nabeskus went on taking the best for herself, giving the leanest and poorest of everything to the woman who had befriended her and taken her into her home.

One day an old man was passing the wigwam and, watching from a distance, he saw what was going on. Just before the next meal time, he went to the spring from which the women got water. Soon Sakum, feeling her way along a length of spruce-twine tied from tree to tree, came to fill the water pot.

"Sakum," he said, "I have that which may be of use to you," and he placed something in her hand. "Rub this on your eyes and you will see again."

Sakum did so, and in a moment could see as well as ever, but when she looked for the old man, he was gone. Then she knew she had spoken with Glooscap, and she thanked him in her heart. She went back to the lodge, touching the twine as she went, out of habit, and found Nabeskus putting down a fine mess of venison at the door. Nearby was a basket of fresh salmon and a large container of maple sugar.

"Not much luck today," said the sly woman.

Puzzled by these words and by the abundance of food, the Chief's wife decided to say nothing for the present about recovering her eyesight She sat down in her usual place and waited for Nabeskus to prepare the meal.

Presently Nabeskus came with a small dish of meat, rather dry and mostly bones, and a cup of cold water which she placed in front of Sakum.

"There you are. Enjoy your meal."

Sakum watched Nabeskus help herself to a dish of fat venison and some fresh-cooked salmon, saw her fill her cup liberally with hot water and sweeten it with maple sugar.

"Why don't you eat?" asked Nabeskus, seeing the Chief's wife had not yet touched her meal. "Not the best meat in the world, I'm afraid, but the best I can find for you today." And she fell upon her own delicious meal with relish.

117

"I see you have done well for *yourself*," said Sakum dryly and the other woman glanced up in surprise. Then, seeing the eyes of the Chief's wife fixed on her with stern reproach, she knew that all was clear as day to Sakum. With a cry of alarm, she cried hastily, "What a mistake I have made! I gave you the wrong dish. Here you are." She hastily set her own dish before Sakum. "You know I always give you the best!" And she took the bones and cold water for herself. The Chief's wife, however, was not deceived.

At that moment Lox came strolling by, still in his raccoon form, and seeing the two women, he thought of another trick to set them fighting. He had learned of Sakum's blindness and had not the least regret for causing it. He assumed she was still blind and therefore took no trouble to keep out of her sight. Going to the pot of venison on the fire, he took out a handful of the meat and threw it at Nabeskus when her head was partly turned away. She, thinking Sakum had taken this method of getting even, began to sob and wail.

"I'm sorry—I won't do it again! Don't be cross with me. I'll eat the worst of everything from now on!"

Sakum was paying no attention. She had seen the raccoon dash up a tree and knew he was up there now, seated on a branch laughing at them. She went to the fire and got some burning sticks, laid them under the tree and added fresh wood. The flames blazed up. Lox, feeling the heat and smelling the smoke, climbed higher but Sakum added fuel to the fire. Now the flames were reaching him no matter how high he climbed, and he was coughing and choking and using very bad language.

"That's the fellow who threw the meat," said Sakum to Nabeskus, who was staring, open-mouthed, and she piled on more wood. This was too much for Lox, so he turned himself into a crow and, cawing angrily, flew away. It is said he was never more seen in that part of the land of the Wabanaki!

The Chief's wife forgave her companion and lived with her in peace, knowing that by keeping two good eyes wide open, neither Lox nor Nabeskus would fool her again.

And so—*kespeadooksit.*

The Chenoo Who
Stayed to Dinner

In the Old Time, a couple named Toma and Nesoowa, newly wed, left their native village and went to hunt in a wild and lonely part of the North Woods.

One day when Nesoowa was alone in the camp, she heard a rustling in the bushes close by as if some wild beast were thrusting its way through. She looked out of the wigwam and saw something so terrible her blood seemed to freeze in her veins. A gaunt old man clothed in moss and leaves and pine needles, his eyes like the eyes of a wolf, came staggering toward her. A Chenoo! (Chenoos, the Wabanaki believed, were humans who had gone mad through evil and become cannibals. Few had seeen these horrors of the North, but it was known that they rubbed their bodies with fir balsam, then rolled on the ground so that everything stuck to them—moss, sticks, leaves, even small stones—and this was how Nesoowa knew what the creature was.)

Alone, without weapon of any kind—and what weapon was any good against a Chenoo?—Nesoowa fell back on what she had, her woman's wit. Instead of showing fear, she approached the Chenoo and addressed him with every appearance of joy.

"My dear father! Where have you come from? Why have you been so long?"

The Chenoo had expected screams and prayers and weeping. Such a welcome confused him and checked his natural instincts. In dull wonder he let Nesoowa lead him to the lodge.

"Wash yourself in the brook, dear father," said Nesoowa tenderly, "then I shall give you a suit of your son-in-law's clothing. You look very ill and tired." And in truth he did, for he had just fought a hard battle with another of his kind—a Chenoo named Winsit—and had barely escaped with his life. Sick as he was and amazed at the attitude of Nesoowa, he did as she told him, cleansed himself in the stream nearby, then put on Toma's clothes and sat far back in the wigwam away from the heat, for being a Northman he liked cold better. Yet his face was still ugly with hate. When she offered him food, he would have none of it. Nesoowa thought of Toma, due to return soon from hunting, wanting to warn him. "I shall get some wood for the fire," she said, but with a surly look he got up and followed her.

"Now my death is near," thought Nesoowa.

"Give me the axe," said the Chenoo, and she dared not refuse him.

"Now, surely," she thought, "this is the end."

But the old man began to chop down trees. Never had Nesoowa seen such chopping. The great pines fell left and right like summer rain. The boughs were hewn and split as if by a tempest. The Chenoo was showing her that, sick as he was, he was still strong. He still held her life in his hands.

"My father," she cried, seeing the woods diminish. "That is enough!"

As the Chenoo laid down the axe, Nesoowa heard a call from the woods—it was Toma. "It is your son-in-law," she told the Chenoo with every appearance of composure. "How pleased he will be to see you," and she hurried to meet her husband, calling out to him that her father had come to visit. Toma, seeing a strange mad-eyed man in the doorway of his lodge, was mystified but, trusting in his wife's wit and common sense, he fell in with the deception.

"Welcome, father-in-law," he said pleasantly. "Come in. Come up to the highest place. I have a pipe for you."

The Chenoo scowled with amazement.

"My husband will have much to tell you," said Nesoowa, "while I prepare our evening meal." The young man sat down beside the Chenoo and began to relate all the events of the day and all that had happened to his wife and himself in recent weeks, and also many things that had never happened at all, simply to keep talking. The Chenoo refused tobacco and food, but listened and, soothed by Toma's voice, presently fell asleep.

Nesoowa, in a whisper, told her husband all that had occurred in his absence. Not daring to move, they sat near their sleeping guest all night, watching. The Chenoo woke in the morning, still grim and silent, still refusing to eat. For three days this continued and one of the couple always watched while the other slept. On the third day the Chenoo spoke.

"Give me tallow," he said shortly.

"Yes, my father," Nesoowa got up quickly.

"Bring a large kettle full and put it on the fire."

Nesoowa did so and when the marrow-fat of the moose was scalding hot, the Chenoo drank it off in one draught.

"Now I shall eat," he said. He was still a Chenoo, with the icy heart and cannibal instincts of his kind, but he had yielded somewhat to the power of kindness, which is sometimes a power quite as strong as magic. He had made up his mind to partake of their hospitality as a sign that he no longer meant them harm. After eating, he lay down and slept. And so, thankfully, did Toma and his wife.

The Chenoo stayed with them all winter. He told them his name was Elaak (meaning "harmful") and his heart had turned to ice only a short time ago. A Chenoo's evil strength, he said, depended on the size and number of hearts he had eaten, so although Elaak was strong and could, in battle, make himself as tall as the highest pine, yet he was weaker than Winsit at the moment, for he, Elaak, had never eaten the heart of another Chenoo.

"I shall eat one some day," said he with a strange inward look, causing all their fears to revive. "Then I shall have my full strength! Meanwhile, I will live with you. Winsit will not think to look for me in the lodge of an Indian."

"You are welcome, my father-in-law," said Toma with a sigh. Fearing to leave his wife alone with the Chenoo, he was unable to go hunting. They had to live almost altogether on stores of dried meat and smoked fish. Elaak soon tired of such fare. "I know a place where fresh meat may be had. Come with me tomorrow, son-in-law, and I will show you some hunting."

Toma had to agree. Nesoowa made the old Chenoo a pair of snowshoes of ashwood, cut green and bent to shape over the heat of the fire, all strung with cords of rawhide and sinew. Both were amazed when Elaak, having put them on, began to move over the snowy trail like the wind. Toma, a young and vigorous man, could barely keep up with the wasted old man.

They came at last to a spring in the woods, and there the snow was melted away around it, showing the grass all flat and green. Elaak removed his snowshoes and began to dance. Soon the water began to heave and boil. Then up came a monstrous creature with a sinuously-waving head, which Elaak cut off with a single blow.

"A lizard!" Toma swallowed hard. He had never seen one before, but large or small, he didn't want to eat one. Indians would eat most things to be found in the woods and in the sea, but not reptiles.

"I conjured it up," said the old man with pride, "from a small spring lizard." He had already made a temendous fire and roasted the meat over it. "Eat!"

Toma's stomach turned, yet he did not dare offend his powerful "father-in-law." He tasted a bit and was surprised. It was like bear's meat and quite tender.

"Cast the head, feet, and tail back in the spring," said the Chenoo as he bound together the rest of the cooked meat and shouldered the burden. "They will grow again into a new lizard. Come, let us go home now to my daughter," and away he went like a bird. The load was nothing to him. Toma was a great runner, yet he soon found himself falling behind.

"Can't you go faster?" asked the Chenoo.

"No!" gasped Toma.

"Then get on my shoulders."

Toma mounted to the top of the load of meat and the old man set off at such a pace that the bushes fairly whistled as they flew past. They were home long before dark.

Then one day when Spring was making the land green,

125

Elaak came to Toma with a hard look in his eyes. "Kaka-kooch the crow tells me that Winsit has found my hiding place. He will soon be here. I must fight him and this time one of us will die." He explained that Chenoos on the way to battle sounded a war whoop so horrible that humans coud die hearing it. The sound was as loud as thunder, as sharp and shrill as the scream of a loon, and it could pierce the brain like an arrow. "There is a cave nearby where you must hide and stop up your ears with moss. Now fetch me my bundle."

Nesoowa brought the bundle the Chenoo had brought with him when he came, which had hung untouched all winter on a tree. Elaak reached in and brought forth a pair of dragon horns, golden bright, one with two branches, the other straight and smooth. He gave the straight one to Toma.

"There is magic in it," said Elaak. "If ever you are near death from a Chenoo, thrust it into his ear and it will kill him. I thank you for making me welcome in your home."

Now Elaak made himself as tall as the tallest pine, up-rooting a smaller tree to use as a club, and there was nothing left but to wait for the foe. Toma drew Nesoowa aside and whispered, "Wife, now that we have the means of destroying a Chenoo, we must use it. If Elaak is the loser, we will use it against Winsit. If Winsit dies in the fight, then we must kill Elaak."

Nesoowa caught her breath.

126

"Kill Elaak?" Without realizing it, she had grown fond of the old man.

"We must," said Toma. "He is a Chenoo, remember, and with them the winner always eats the loser's heart. If Elaak eats Winsit's, he will become more evil than ever and eat ours next!"

Nesoowa saw with dismay that this was so. Yet the thought of killing the old man who had shared their lodge for so long was painful. An Indian woman seldom argues with her husband, so she made no outward objection, only went a little way off in the woods and sent a silent message to Glooscap.

Because her heart was brave and loving, Glooscap heard and came in the shape of a Canada jay, alighting on the branch of a spruce. "Take the plant you see growing at your feet." Nesoowa looked and saw a plant with a bright red flower, one she had never seen before. She plucked it. "Grind the blossom and mix it with water. If Elaak survives the fight, it will be up to you to use your woman's wit to make him drink it."

A shout came from Toma. "Hurry, wife! Come quickly! We must hide."

Nesoowa turned to thank Glooscap, but the jay had flown. She ran to join Toma in the cave, where they stopped their ears with moss and waited. Soon their ears began to sting painfully. The whoop of Winsit was so long and awful it was like nothing on earth, and when it ended the

couple felt weak. Now they could hear the sounds of a tremendous battle, which went on for a long time. At last Toma could stand the suspense no longer. "I must go and see what is happening."

"I'll come with you," said Nesoowa and the two crept out of the quiet cave into a noisy world of flying earth clods, rocks, and tree branches. What they saw was frightening. The two Chenoos, each as tall as a pine, were locked in fierce embrace. Winsit had taken Elaak's branched horn and was slowly pushing the old man backwards. As Elaak fell, the ground shook, rocks crashed down, and the breath of Winsit was like a forest fire. "Now I'll take your life," he roared, "and eat your heart!" He tried to drive the golden horn into Elaak's head, but the old man moved his head rapidly from side to side to avoid the thrust.

"Help!" cried Elaak, desperately.

"Who would help you?" mocked Winsit. "Who cares if you live or die?"

Now Toma, who was so small beside these giants that the evil Winsit never even noticed him, suddenly found that he too cared what happened to the old man he had called "father-in-law," and without stopping to think, he drove his single golden horn into Winsit's ear. It lengthened as it entered, darting through Winsit's head and out the other side, killing him instantly.

Elaak staggered to his feet and cried with fierce delight, "I have won! Now I shall eat his heart!"

129

"Wait!" cried Nesoowa, offering him a birchbark cup. "You must be thirsty, my father! Drink this first."

Elaak snatched the cup and swallowed the contents.

A moment he stood, staring at them with angry reddened eyes. Then, gradually, his expression changed. He seemed dazed. His shoulders drooped. He shrank back to his normal size, and became just an ordinary, tired old man. "My children," he said with a gentle smile, "help me to bed."

From that day on, Elaak lived with Toma and Nesoowa in peace, and when children came to the young couple he was the kindest of grandfathers. They were troubled no more by Chenoos of any size or description.

And so—*kespeadooksit.*

Glooscap, the
Peacemaker

GLOOSCAP WAS SAD because his Malicetes and his Penobscots, children of the same family, were at war with each
other. And this was how it had come about.

The Malicetes were expert beaver hunters and got more
skins each year than they needed for their own use. The
Penobscots were exceptionally good bead and arrow makers
and made more than enough for themselves. The two
tribes therefore met each Spring and Autumn to trade their
surplus goods. After one of these trading operations, hosts
and visitors were celebrating with a feast and games. In one
of the rougher games, a Penobscot boy was accidentally
knocked down and later died of his injury. The Penobscots
agreed that it was an accident, but it was remembered, and
when the tribes met in Penobscot territory the following

131

Spring, a group of vengeful youths took advantage of a mock battle to slay two Malicete boys. This too was passed over as an accident, but the Malicetes knew it had been deliberate and they nursed their hatred until an opportunity came for revenge. At salmon time, they descended upon a Penobscot fishing party and killed every one. From then on, the two tribes were sworn enemies.

One Autumn day a war party of a hundred Penobscots rushed down by river upon an unsuspecting Malicete village while the men were away hunting. At the far end of the village, a woman named Kogun snatched up her baby, ran to the river and hid him in the cattails, then walked out proudly to meet the tomahawks of the enemy. The Penobscot Chief, seeing that the woman was courageous as well as comely, ordered his braves to take her prisoner, thinking she would make a good servant for his wife. So the Penobscots bound Kogun's arms and led her into the Chief's canoe. When all their deadly work was done, they embarked again downstream.

The lower tributaries of the Oolastuk, however, were unfamiliar to the Penobscots and they moved slowly, avoiding side streams for fear of hidden rocks and shallows. The Malicete woman soon perceived the uneasiness of the enemy and thought of a scheme to take advantage of it. Kogun, whose name means "froth on the water" had been given that name because she was an unusually fine swimmer, and this accomplishment she decided to make use of in her plan.

"I know the river," she told the Penobscot Chief. "I do not wish to be upset in the rapids and drown, so I will show you the way if you will unbind me."

The matter was debated. Some wished to stop and camp where they were until daylight, but the Chief argued that they should put as much distance as possible between themselves and the Malicetes. At last it was decided to go on, and since among so many there seemed no chance for the woman to escape, they untied Kogun and told her to guide them. "Treachery will mean your death," the Chief said. "Is the river dangerous?"

"Not if you follow the right streams," she answered, resolved to see that they took the wrong ones. She knew too that the Great Falls lay just ahead.

Suspecting nothing, the Penobscots paddled their war canoes with more confidence. At the next fork, Kogun knew they must take the stream to the left in order to avoid the Falls, but when the Chief asked, "Which way?" she answered steadily, "To the right."

In the darkness they drew closer and closer to the danger point, and the sound of many paddles covered the warning mutter of rapids. One man, however, was uneasy.

"Is all well?"

"All is well. Keep on!"

The river took a sharp turn. They were nearly there! Kogun saw white water ahead, gleaming in the moonlight, but in their sleepy state the paddlers did not notice. Kogun waited no longer but, swift as an otter, dove over the side of the canoe. As she swam with all her strength toward shore, she heard the cries of her former captors as they were swept to their death over the Great Falls.

Only a few were actually lost, for the following canoes were able to back water and turn toward land. They reached calm water at the river's edge just as Kogun herself reached it. With shouts of rage, the Penobscots leaped out, pursued and caught her. She was carried up on dry land, a prisoner again. The furious Penobscots, saying a quick death would be too good for the woman who had caused the destruction of twenty men including their Chief, decided to carry her a close prisoner back to their own country. They would decide there what was to be done with her.

Meanwhile, back at Kogun's village, the men had returned from hunting to find their homes in ruins, many of their people dead or wounded. Those who survived told Wejebok, the husband of Kogun, that his child was safe but his wife carried off a prisoner. Desolate and angry, Wejebok vowed to go after her.

"The enemy will be a long way down the river by now." a friend argued, "perhaps even back in their own country."

"Even if we could catch up with them," said another, "they would be too many for us."

But Wejebok closed his ears to reason.

"I must find my wife. I shall go alone."

Shamed by his courage, five young men, who had no families of their own, agreed to go with him.

The six traveled all that evening and came at length to the Falls. One of the Malicetes shouted and pointed to a piece of broken canoe floating in the rapids.

"They must have gone over. It is no use to go farther."

But Wejebok looked at a path freshly made through the woods.

"A large party has gone through, carrying canoes. If there were survivors, they would have to portage here and so come to the river again below the Falls. Stay here while I scout ahead and see what I can find."

Wejebok moved swiftly and silently along the path until he reached a hill where he could look down on the enemy camped below. He saw his wife, bound to a tree, alive and unharmed.

The new Chief had decided to risk camping below the Falls for the night, dreading to go on in darkness along an unknown river. After all, he reasoned, they still numbered eighty braves and had no real fear of the Malicetes.

Wejebok from his watching post counted the Penobscots and felt despair. How could he get his wife away from eighty watchful enemies? In his distress, he thought of Glooscap—remembering that the Lord of Men and Beasts had promised always to help his people in time of need.

"O Great Chief," he whispered, "help me save my wife."

Even as the words took shape in his mind, a great eagle

soared down from the night sky, alighting on a branch near Wejebok. "If you do exactly as I say, and if you promise not to seek revenge thereafter, but strive for peace, all will be well." Wejebok knew at once that this was the voice of the Master and gave his promise gladly.

"Tomorrow when it is light," the voice went on, "you must start from the far end of that island and paddle up past the enemy's camp. Your three canoes will pass the camp one at a time, and *land* one at a time on the island. You will then carry your canoes one at a time into the trees out of sight, across to the other side of the island, where you will launch them again."

Wejebok began to see what the Great Chief had in mind and smiled exultantly. It was just the sort of strategy an Indian admired.

"If you keep repeating this over and over," said the Master, "it will seem to the Penobscots that hundreds of canoes are landing to mass for battle. You will know what to do after that, but remember—seek no revenge! Make peace!" And Wejebok heard the rustle of wings as the eagle flew off through the trees.

Wejebok returned to his friends and explained the plan. They lifted their canoes and, cautiously skirting the Penobscot camp, they set them down again in the water downstream of the enemy. There they crossed to the island and waited for dawn.

As soon as it was light, Wejebok and one companion

paddled out around the end of the island. The enemy's scouts saw them and woke the rest of the camp, who, rushing down to the shore to look, assumed it had come down the river. In great excitement they were preparing to launch their canoes when—

"Look!" someone cried, and they saw a second craft appear.

The Penobscots decided to wait a moment and learn the full strength of the Malicete war party.

By this time, the leading canoe had landed and was being carried out of sight among the trees on the island. Moments later, the second was drawn up on shore and hoisted on Malicete shoulders. Just as the third canoe had arrived and disappeared in the same way, a fourth canoe came around the bend. The distance was too great for the Penobscots to see that the men in the canoe were the same as those in the first one, and that this was Wejebok making a second trip.

Now the Penobscots began to feel worried. As they watched and counted, six—ten—twenty—*thirty* Malicete canoes seemed to pass and land. And more! Where had they all come from? All morning and all afternoon the three canoes passed and repassed, and after dark they still came, their ghostly shapes lit by the light of torches. With two men to each canoe, the Penobscots counted a hundred and sixty men.

"We are outnumbered," groaned the Penobscots, "there

is only one thing to do—sue for peace!"

With a bitter heart, sure that the Malicete terms would be high, the Chief's son ordered Kogun released and placed in his canoe as a pledge of good faith. Then he paddled to the island, making signs that he wished a peace parley. Wejebok saw him coming, saw his wife in the bow, and rejoiced in his heart. He walked to meet the Penobscot with an air of cold dignity, however, trying to look like the Chief of a mighty host.

The two met on the shore and seated themselves over a peace pipe to discuss terms of surrender.

"It was in my mind to destroy your whole army," said Wejebok darkly, "but last night our Great Chief Glooscap came to me and said he desired peace between us. Let us bury the hatchet."

Hardly believing in his good fortune, the Penobscot agreed. The pipe of peace was smoked and the two great war parties separated without actually counting each others' numbers!

Far away on the summit of Blomidon, Glooscap smoked, content. The war had been ended without bloodshed. His people were at peace again.

And *kespeadooksit*—the story ends.

The Strongest Boy
in the World

ONCE IN THE Old Time, an orphaned boy named Sabadis
went to live with his uncle, a man too cross and lazy to get
a wife and too mean to hire a housekeeper, which is why
he was willing to adopt a strong boy like Sabadis who could
do his work for him.

The lodge of Sabadis and his uncle stood behind a great
rock pile which got in the way of the view. The uncle, being stupid as well as lazy, instead of moving the wigwam
to a better place gave Sabadis the task of removing the rock
pile, stone by stone. Sabadis, the opposite of his uncle in all
things, made no complaint but cheerfully did as he was
told. Being strong to begin with, the work made him
stronger, and by the time the job was done, Sabadis was
seven times as strong as his uncle and might easily—if he

140

had wanted to—have tossed the old man into the river. Since Sabadis was as gentle as he was strong, the thought never occurred to him.

It was some time before the uncle noticed what had happened to his nephew. Then one day he saw the boy lift a huge tree trunk and toss it aside as if it were a chip. Then he noticed how the village people had got in the habit of coming to watch Sabadis as he did his work, and this made him think of a way to make more profit from the boy.

"We will travel about the land of the Wabanaki," he told Sabadis, "and I will show the people the Strongest Boy in the World. Wherever we go, we will be welcomed and fed and I shall not have the trouble of hunting any more. Come, boy, pack up the wigwam. Put food in the canoe."

"No, Uncle," said Sabadis quietly, and the answer shocked the uncle so much he lost his breath for a moment.

"You disobey me?" he gasped.

"I'm sorry, but I do not care to be shown off before strangers," said the boy. "Nor can I stay here where people think my strength peculiar and, fearing it, deny me their fellowship. I must go out into the world and find friends of my own." And he walked away.

"Come back!" shouted the angry man, hurling sticks and stones after him, but the boy took no notice and soon was lost to sight. And after that the uncle had to get his living by himself for a change.

Sabadis walked on, with hope for company. He had

always been lonely. Now, soon, he might find a friend.

He traveled for many days and came at last to where the land showed itself like a bowstring along the sea. Here he paused to watch a tall man lift a canoe with many people in it. When the man had got it above his head, he grinned and dropped it, people and all, and if Sabadis had not waded in and picked them out of the water, they would all have been lost.

This man was strong. Perhaps, thought Sabadis, he is the one I have been looking for. "Will you be my friend?" he asked the man.

Now the man, whose name was Wiskum, would not have troubled himself with the friendship of a boy, yet having seen Sabadis' strength and quickness, he did not like to say no. So they went along together and Sabadis thought to himself, happily, "What pleasure there is in friendship!"

The next day they saw a man rolling a mighty rock up a hill, and when he had got it to the top he purposely let it go. It rolled down toward the village and would certainly have killed all the people if Sabadis had not caught the rock in time and tossed it into the lake. The man's surprise was great, to see such strength in a mere boy.

"Will you too be my friend?" asked the strong boy, "and travel along with us?"

"All right," said the man, who said his name was Woltes. "I don't mind if I do."

And they all went along together, Sabadis joyful in his new-found friends, sure he would never be lonely again. They came at length to a hardwood ridge where they decided to make camp. A hardwood ridge is always a good place for Indians to live, for it provides plenty of birch, ash, and other woods useful in making housekeeping articles.

The morning after their arrival, Sabadis and Wiskum went hunting, leaving Woltes in charge of the camp and the cooking. Just as the sun was at the edge of noon, the one who had been left in camp looked out the door and saw a stranger, a small hairy boy, very thin and wretched looking. He wore a belt much too large for him.

"Give me food quickly," begged the boy, "for I starve!" And indeed he looked as though he had not had a meal in many days.

"Be off!" said the strong man roughly. "There's only enough for ourselves."

The elf-boy laughed, went to the fire and helped himself, while Woltes by some strange enchantment found himself rooted to the ground, without even the power of speech. The boy ate all the dinner there was, all the stew prepared for three, not leaving a scrap. Then he simply walked into the hardwood ridge the way a man might walk into fog, and vanished. Woltes found he could move and speak again, only now it was too late. He spent his fury in shouting useless threats and overturning the pot on the fire. When the others returned and heard why there was no dinner, they could scarcely believe him.

"A likely story!" shouted Wiskum. "You ate all the food yourself." And if Sabadis had not stepped between them, there would have been broken heads.

The next day the Strongest Boy in the World and Woltes went hunting, leaving Wiskum at home. He had just got the venison simmering nicely when the little fellow appeared again, quietly from nowhere.

"Please give me something to eat, for I am starving."

"Oh no you don't," said Wiskum. "Stay away from that pot!" But suddenly he was as if bolted to the earth and had to stand and watch in bitter silence while the boy disposed of the food. Having eaten the last bit, the boy laughed and vanished into the ridge, leaving the man free again but in such a temper he danced and tore his hair. When he told the other two that night, he had to listen to the taunts of Woltes, and again Sabadis was obliged to make peace between them.

On the third day, it was Sabadis' turn to stay in camp.

"Watch out for the boy," they warned him.

Sabadis prepared the meal and waited—and sure enough, just at noon the starving child came and began to beg piteously. "I am starving. Please give me food!"

"Very well," said Sabadis, "the pot is full. Help yourself, but eat as others eat, and no tricks!"

The boy grinned.

"No tricks, very well. But I cannot eat as others eat. I

must eat all. Stop me if you can." And he reached for the food. No bonds held Sabadis as they had the others, and he rushed at the elf. They wrestled for possession of the pot and Sabadis was amazed to find that this thin and weak-looking boy was his equal in strength. Struggling with him, he felt the excitement and pleasure of contesting with an equal. Face to face, laughing, the two fought until the sun was low in the sky and at last the elf-boy cried, "Enough! We are well matched. You may keep your food."

"Who are you?" demanded Sabadis, seeing there was more to this boy than he had at first suspected.

"I am Marten, the *megumoowesoo,*" the boy answered, "the servant of Glooscap, who sent me to test your strength, your courage and kindness. Now ask what you wish and, by the power of Glooscap's belt which I wear, I can give it to you."

"Be my friend," said Sabadis eagerly, but Marten shook his head, with regret.

"We are of different worlds. Would a sister do instead?"

Sabadis was disappointed but tried not to show it.

"I have never had a sister," he admitted. "Thank you."

"Follow me," said the little *megumoowesoo,* and he walked straight into the ridge. Sabadis, anticipating a painful collision, shut his eyes but it proved an unnecessary precaution, for he easily followed the boy through rock and wood and entered a vast cave. There Marten put fine new doeskin garments on Sabadis and led him to an inner cave

146

where a girl his own age, very slender and delicate, waited shyly.

"This is your sister," said Marten. "Her name is Welahe."

"My friends will want a sister too," said Sabadis.

"They must want," said Marten. "Beware, Sabadis, of easy friendships, and never trust your life to ones so fond of death." Saying this, he gave a leap into the air, spun around three times, and vanished.

"Come, my brother," said Welahe, "I will show you the way," and she led Sabadis out through an invisible door.

It had seemed only a moment to Sabadis that he had been in the cave, yet on looking around he saw that the camp was deserted. The two men had gone, taking weapons, food, and implements with them, his as well as their own. The ashes of the fire were cold, but not yet disturbed by wind or rain, so the men could not have been long gone.

"They have taken my blanket and food with them," said Sabadis, "so that being less burdened I can soon catch up with them."

Welahe said nothing. She loved this gentle youth already and did not like to disagree with him, but it seemed to her that taking a man's blanket and food was not the act of honest men. Sabadis studied the tracks on the ground. "They have gone toward the great cliff. Come, we must hurry to catch up."

Before the sun reached the horizon, they arrived at the

bottom of the cliff, and Sabadis saw dim figures standing on top. "Wiskum—Woltes! Wait for me!"

"Is that you, Sabadis?" he heard Wiskum's voice call down in surprise. "We thought you were lost!"

"Don't take the path," shouted Woltes. "It will be quicker if we send down a rope and haul you up."

"Very well," agreed the Strongest Boy in the World. He could barely see the men now, and they could not see him and Welahe at all, due to the cliff's overhang. He waited for the rope to descend.

"Tie a stone to the rope," whispered Welahe, "and send it up first."

"No," said the boy. "Such suspicion is unworthy of you, my sister. They are my friends."

"Then let me go up first," she begged.

He hesitated.

"Very well. There is nothing to fear." He made sure she was securely tied to the rope and watched her slight figure move slowly up the face of the cliff. He smiled, thinking how surprised the men would be. Welahe was only a darker shadow now, moving upward, almost to the top. Now it stopped moving, hung motionless for a moment, then—suddenly, with terrible speed, it came tumbling down and Welahe was dashed to pieces on the ground. As Sabadis stood frozen with horror, he heard Wiskum's voice drift down from the cliff top. "That's done it."

"Yes, "said Woltes. "We're rid of the boy at last."

Then Sabadis knew that neither of the men had been his friend, and that the only one who had really cared for him was dead. "Welahe," he wept, "my sister—my friend!"

"Yes," said the voice of Marten, "she was your friend."

Sabadis turned with leaping hope to the little *megumoowesoo*. "But Glooscap can bring her to life again!"

"Not to this life," said Marten slowly, and he smiled at Sabadis. "This world is not ready yet for two of your sort. I shall take you to a better place." And touching the great belt at his waist, Marten wished them all in the back of the Northland in a lodge at the end of the sky.

"Arise now, Welahe, and make arrows for your brother."

Then Welahe arose, as lovely as ever. She smiled at her brother and Sabadis knew he would never be lonely again.

And since that day, whenever colored spears of light shoot in splendor out of a dark Autumn sky, most people say "Ah, the Northern Lights," but the Indians know better.

"It is the Strongest Boy in the World," they say, "shooting the arrows made by his sister."

And so—*kespeadooksit*—another tale is over.

The Magic
Snowshoes

In a Huron camp beside the river Hochelaga, there lived a Micmac boy and his mother, taken prisoner a dozen years before. The boy, whose name was Wokun, was a baby when captured and could not even remember his homeland.

"Some day when you are a grown man," said his mother, "we will escape and return to the Micmac country."

It seemed to Wokun that growing up would take forever. Meanwhile he was the butt of all the jokes and games in the Huron camp.

"Porcupine eater! Only poor ignorant Micmacs eat porcupine!"

It was no good saying that one didn't eat the quills and that, according to his mother, porcupine meat was very

150

good, provided it was cooked properly. The important thing was to bear all and make no outcry or complaint or they would deem him a coward and make his life even more miserable.

Wokun's only happy times were with his mother alone in the woods when they were sent to cut up the hunters' game. There they could talk freely of the home he had never seen and of the great hero, Glooscap, who watched over his Wabanaki and helped them when they were in trouble.

"Blomidon is a long way off," sighed Wokun. "Glooscap has forgotten us."

"Not so," said his mother. "He will help us when we really need him. We must first do all we can to show by our courage and industry that we deserve his help."

So she showed him how to practice blowing feathers and outrunning them in order to grow swift-footed, how to pound up fish bones to dust and blow them against the wind to make his lungs strong. She made him a map of the Wabanaki country and taught him the history and language of his own people. She even made him a miniature Micmac moccasin and pressed it in the ground so Wokun would recognize its shape if ever he saw it on the trail. The boy looked around at the quiet forest and cried longingly, "Why can't we run away now?"

"The enemy would soon catch us and bring us back." said his mother, "to worse trials and closer imprisonment.

It is a long way to our own country, my son, and our people fear the Huron. We must be quiet and lull their suspicions until the time comes."

Events, however, crowded down on Wokun that very day. Back in camp, the Huron Chief caught the boy's mother in some fancied wrong and began to beat her. Wokun rushed to his mother's defense and in his wild fury knocked the Chief down, adding insult to injury by cutting off his scalp lock while he lay unconscious.

"Now all is lost," his mother moaned, as the Hurons dragged her son to a post in the center of the camp and tied him there, promising he would be put to death on the following day. The Huron boys threw stones at him, but Wokun did not cry out, not once, and at last they tired of the sport and went to their lodges to sleep.

When all was still, Wokun wept quietly in the darkness, not for his hurts nor for the thought of tomorrow, but because now he would never grow up to see his own country and take his mother back to it. He hardly heard the soft rush of air close by, or the rustle of feathers, until a giant grey heron settled on the ground and he heard it speak.

"Well done, Wokun!"

The boy expected the whole camp to waken at the thunderous voice, yet no one even stirred. Then he guessed that he and only he could hear the voice.

"Glooscap?" he asked, trembling between hope and fear.

The heron nodded gravely.

"You have honored me and your people with your courage."

"Oh, Master, help us get back to our own country!"

"Breathe in three times," commanded the Lord of Men and Beasts, and Wokun obeyed. Once, twice, thrice, and with each breath he grew larger until at last his bonds snapped and he stood free.

"Thank you, Master!"

Then Glooscap told him to go to his mother and say he must leave without her.

"Your mother is too old to travel as you must travel. She will be safe, I promise you. Tell her you will return with help as soon as you find your own people. When I am gone, break that stick on the ground and it will become a pair of snowshoes. With them you can travel over ice or snow, under the snow, and even through the treetops." And with a rush of his great wings, he was gone.

Wokun did all that Glooscap had told him. Then, putting on the magic snowshoes, he set off at top speed. When dawn lighted the camp a short time later, the Hurons saw that their prisoner had escaped, and started in furious pursuit, confident they would catch him easily before he reached the river. If not, however, the river would surely stop him. At this time of year, it was only partly frozen and full of floating ice cakes. To cross, it was necessary to haul the canoes up on the ice every so often and carry them to the next stretch of open water, and this work called for two strong men.

But Wokun, with his magic snowshoes, needed no canoe! The astounded Hurons saw him leap from shore and land squarely on the nearest ice cake, and even as they launched their canoes, Wokun was halfway across, leaping from cake to cake on his marvelous footgear. Who would have imagined that one who was a boy only yesterday now traveled faster than a man!

The Hurons reached the other side with the utmost difficulty and donning their own snowshoes, set off again in pursuit. When they were almost upon him, to their fresh astonishment Wokun dove under the snow, snowshoes and all!

"Now we have him!" they shouted after they got over their surprise. And they thrust their spears in the snow here, there, and everywhere—but no matter where they thrust or poked, Wokun wasn't there.

The young Micmac traveled along under the snow for some distance before coming up for a breath of air. Looking back, he saw the Hurons waving their spears at him, and laughed. He gave them a mocking wave and sprang to a branch of the nearest tree. From there he leaped to another. This was too much for the Hurons! Seeing a man on snowshoes leap from tree to tree like a squirrel, they lost heart and gave up the chase. They knew magic when they saw it, and who could fight magic? They hurried back to camp to tell their tale, and to cast respectful side glances

154

at the mother of the "magician"—which assured her she was safe from harm thereafter.

Wokun traveled through the treetops until he thought himself beyond reach of the enemy, then dropped to the snowy ground and traveled in the usual way. After some days, the snow began to disappear. Now the land appeared, softly green and pleasant with hills and valleys—beautiful, just as his mother had said. On the soft ground he saw a foot print and studied it. It was the mark of a moccasin, the exact shape of the one made by his mother. He was certainly in Micmac territory at last.

"Down with the Huron!" A great shout, then a chorus of angry yells shattered the silence and he thought for a moment the enemy had caught him.

"Kill him! Kill the Huron!" The words were in his mother's tongue. These were Micmacs!

"I am a Micmac like yourselves," he cried, and seeing them pause, he pulled something from his belt and cast it on the ground. "Look! The scalp lock of a Huron Chief!"

At that sure proof, the Micmacs put away their knives, asking his name and where he came from. Wokun told his story and begged them to return with him to save his mother. At this they frowned and shook their heads. "They are too many for us."

"Not if we can surprise them," pleaded Wokun.

They agreed to consider the matter in council, and each brave spoke his views in turn. At the end, Wokun spoke again.

156

"They are men like ourselves, no stronger, no braver. We can give them such a battle they will never trouble us again. Remember the wrongs they have done us, the women and children taken captive, the young braves slain. Remember how Glooscap helped me in my need and how he will help again if we need him."

Moved by his eloquence, one young brave sprang up and began to stamp his feet in approval. Then all the rest joined in. The war dance was performed and then they set out for the country of the Huron with Wokun as guide.

Winter had settled in around the Huron country. Rivers and lakes were hard under a blanket of snow, but this was good, for, on snowshoes, they could move quickly. When they reached the great river, they found it solidly frozen and crossed at night without difficulty. So rapidly and silently did they approach, the Hurons were taken completely by surprise. With shrilling war cries, Wokun and the Micmacs stormed the palisades and overwhelmed the enemy within. Seeing Wokun of the supernatural snowshoes, the Hurons' courage was shaken and they gave up after a short struggle.

So Wokun's mother was carried back in triumph to her own land and the Micmacs marveled at the great power and goodness of Glooscap who watched over his people and helped them, even when they were far from home.

And now—*kespeadooksit*—the story ends.

Pulowech, the Partridge

PULOWECH the partridge and Teetees the jay were next-door neighbors. The partridge was the steady, respectable sort who worked hard and never took a vacation. Teetees on the other hand was a handsome light-hearted fellow who never let work interfere with fun. Neither was married. Teetees lived alone, but Pulowech had a grandmother who took care of him.

All went well between the two until the day the partridge said to his grandmother, "Don't invite the jay to dinner tonight."

"Why not?"

"He comes too often. Let him eat somewhere else for a change. Why should I always feed him who never feeds me, and seldom says thank-you when I do. Tell him there's

158

nothing in the house to eat."

"Very well," said the old lady, "but I broke my kettle today and if I'm to cook your dinner I must borrow the jay's. He'll wonder why I want it if there's nothing to cook."

"Let him wonder," grunted Pulowech. "Just be sure to wash the pot clean afterward so he won't taste or smell what was in it." Generally hospitable, Pulowech had for some time past been growing annoyed with the jay, calling him in his mind *"moalet,"* meaning "one who lives off his neighbors."

"If *you* wanted anything," said Noogumee, his grandmother, "I'm sure he'd give it to you."

"No doubt!" snapped Pulowech, "if he had it to give! And how can he ever have anything to give when, instead of working hard as I do, he gads about with friends all the time? It's all very well to be generous, but when people take to living off you—" And he went on grumbling like this while Noogumee borrowed the pot and all the while he was eating the good dinner she had cooked in it—only for some reason the meal didn't taste as good as usual.

After supper, his grandmother carefully washed and wiped the pot and carried it back to their neighbor. As she went to hand it over, the lid gave a jump, and both smelled the savory odor of stew. Amazed, the jay lifted the lid, then smiled with pleasure. "What a joker your grandson is—letting on he had nothing to eat, then sending me

159

over this fine dinner! Thanks, Pulowech," Teetees shouted.
"I shall enjoy this."

Pulowech had no idea what Teetees meant, of course,
until Noogumee came rushing home to tell him, and then
he was both puzzled and angry.

"Did you take him dinner after all?"

"Oh no, grandson."

"Then he must have conjured it up by magic," cried
Pulowech excitedly. "He has *keskamzit!*" *Keskamzit,* of
course, was magic power. "Isn't that just like the jay, keeping his *keskamzit* a secret so he can provide good things
just for himself!" And the partridge got himself so worked
up over the jay's greed and secretiveness that at last he
stormed over to Teetees' lodge. "So you have *keskamzit*
and never told me," he shouted. "Isn't it enough that you
live off me, *moalet?* Must you deceive me as well?"

The jay stared at him, open-mouthed.

"What are you talking about, Pulowech?"

"Don't pretend! I know well enough you conjured up
that stew in the kettle just to make me look—to show
me—" Pulowech was having trouble saying what he felt
without revealing his own dishonesty—"to spite me for—"
but he had already said too much.

"Ah-hah!" cried Teetees. "So you lied about having no
meat in the house, and meant me to go hungry!"

"That's right," howled the partridge, "blame everything
on me! When did you last invite me to dinner?"

"What's that got to do with it? You know you can come to my place any time you like! As for my being *moalet,* most people are only too glad to have Teetees dine with them—if only to hear my songs and stories!"

"That's right—boast about your popularity!" Pulowech was so angry now that he trembled. "If you're such a popular fellow, why don't you eat with them instead of me?"

"I will!"

"Good! Stay away from my cooking fire after this!"

The two were enemies after that and avoided each other. Pulowech still believed Teetees had "magicked up" the food with *keskamzit.* Teetees, knowing he hadn't, was puzzled to know who had. He finally decided it was the work of some evil spirit who wanted to make trouble between Teetees and his neighbor. Both were wrong.

"It seems," said Glooscap the Great Chief, "that by putting that food in Teetees' kettle I have only made things worse!"

Now the jay, for all he had boasted of his many friends, was secretly worried, afraid that if Pulowech thought him *moalet,* others might think so too. It might be best to stay away from his friends' homes for a while and do his own hunting and cooking for a change, which he did.

In a very short time, however, the hard work became a nuisance and interferred with his pleasures, so Teetees thought of a new solution—he would get himself a wife.

There being no female jays in the neighborhood, Teetees feared he must go abroad to find one. Then it occurred to him that fairies were said to make good wives for such as himself, if they could be caught and tamed. He had also heard that girls of the fairy sort dwelt in caves under the waters of a lake nearby.

So the jay set out to fish for a wife, and this was the manner of his fishing. He hid behind some rocks hung all over with grapevines and waited until he heard laughing and splashing, then peeped out and saw half a dozen of the fairy girls swimming and playing in the water. A few of them untied their hairstrings and threw them on the bank to dry. Knowing that in her hairstring lay the fairy's power, the jay watched until the girl he most fancied untied hers and threw it on the grass. Then, with a quick dart, Teetees seized it and with a merry whoop flew for home. The fairy who owned it had no choice but to follow, for without her hairstring she could not go back to her own world under the water. When they were some distance from the lake, Teetees stopped and waited in a chestnut tree. When the fairy girl appeared, all out of breath, he held out the hairstring and smiled. "I am tired of living alone," he said, and this is the Indian way of proposing marriage. The girl, glancing sideways at the handsome Teetees, decided against going home after all and promised to remain with him if he would bring one of her sisters to keep her company. Teetees was only too willing, thinking it great sport to catch water fairies, and he soon brought back a sister-in-law who, having lost her hairstring, had no say in the matter.

Now Pulowech, seeing his neighbor come home with not one but two pretty girls to keep house for him, was reminded that he himself had no wife at all. He had Noogumee, but she was not the liveliest company in the world. Anyway, why should Teetees, the lazy one, the sponger, the *moalet,* have so much and he so little?

The partridge learned in a roundabout way how the jay had got the girls and resolved to get one for himself in the same manner. He went to the lake and hid behind the grapevines. At length he beheld the girls jumping and splashing merrily, but the sight so excited him he caught up *all* the hairstrings and made off. Not being as quick as Teetees, he was seen and pursued by the fairy girls. They soon caught up with him and knocked him about so much he dropped every one of the hairstrings, whereupon the girls picked them up and departed, leaving him a widower before he was even a husband! To make matters worse, Teetees—the despicable Teetees who had caused all his troubles—laughed heartily from a tree nearby.

"You should stick to the kind of hunting you know best," the jay chuckled. "Fairies are too much for you."

Pulowech danced with fury.

"You have *keskamzit* to help you. It's not fair! After all the meals you've eaten under my smoke hole, you might have offered one of those girls to me!"

"You told me to stay away from your fire, remember,"

163

Teetees laughed. "So now you can skin your own skunks and catch your own wife. Don't depend on me."

Pulowech seized a stick and sought to persuade Teetees with it, but the jay gave a quick answer by shooting a flint-headed arrow through the other's scalp lock, and in this way the battle continued until a voice of thunder made them fly apart.

"Shame on you both!" And there stood the Great Chief, frowning down at them. "Is this the way for neighbors to

behave? Go home, Teetees, and see to your own affairs."
Nobody stops to argue with Glooscap. The jay flew home
in a hurry.

Glooscap looked at Pulowech, who rushed to defend
himself.

"It was all Teetees' fault, Master. He's a useless fellow
who lives off his neighbors. Yet with his *keskamzit* he is
able to get all the food he wants, and wives as well. He
gives me nothing after all I have done for him."

"Nor should he, if the only reason you gave was to get something back," said Glooscap severely. "Teetees has no *keskamzit*. It was I who put the stew in the pot."

"Oh!" said Pulowech, suddenly feeling as though the ground had been cut from under his feet.

"If you had *keskamzit*, Pulowech, what would you do with it?"

The partridge stared into space for a moment, then scratched his head, embarrassed. "I don't know, Master. I can't think of a thing I need that I haven't already got."

"How about a wife?"

Pulowech was more embarrassed than ever. "Er—I think Noogumee suits me well enough. She knows my ways."

"So you only wanted what Teetees had because he had it," said Glooscap sternly, "as if what made him rich, made you poor. Why?"

Now at last Pulowech understood. He saw in a flash that it hadn't been Teetees' sponging he had minded. He had simply envied the jay his assurance, his popularity, his fine clothes—and the worst of it was, he knew he wouldn't change with the jay if he could. He'd have no peace with two young girls in the house and he hated visiting. He got sleepy early and liked to go to bed. The jay's life would not be to his taste at all!

"It was envy," he admitted, ashamed. "I'm sorry, Master. I was wrong and silly. I see that now."

"Being sorry—is that enough?"

"No, Master," said the partridge meekly, and called out to Noogumee. "Put more food in the pot. That Teetees is such a poor provider. Those wives of his—I don't suppose they get much to eat. We'll have them all to dinner!"

"And so—" the Great Chief smiled. *"Kespeadooksit!"*

Glooscap and the
Seven Wishes

Now THE day came when Glooscap had rid the world of evil beings. *Kookwes* strode across the land no longer, the Culloos were gone from the sky. Not a booöin was left, nor a witch, nor a monster. The Chenoos of the North were no more. The Lord of Men and Beasts had, moreover, through the years taught his people how to live wisely and well. And yet—?

How much had they really learned?

Glooscap sat smoking his great pipe for a long time, thinking deeply, and then he saw a way to test his people's wisdom, courage, and charity.

He sent Kweemoo the loon to all corners of the Wabanaki world to announce that he was moving to a new lodge in the North beyond Gaspé, to an island called

Munagesunook (meaning surf-lashed) and the way to it was very hard and dangerous. Yet whoever came to him there would receive his heart's desire. Each man who succeeded in reaching him would be allowed one wish and it would be granted no matter what it was.

Many tried to find the way to Munagesunook. Some went a long distance before giving up, but in the end their fears betrayed them. Finally, the tribes met in council and chose seven of their strongest and bravest young men to make the attempt. The seven would travel in company and so be able to help each other over the hard places. The usual dances were performed to lull evil spirits to sleep, and tobacco was thrown on the flames in the hope that the good ones would give aid to the travelers. Then the seven young men set off.

There was first of all an exceedingly high mountain. The ascent on one side was steep and smooth with hardly a foothold, and the other side was jagged with rocks. Somehow, helping each other, they managed to pass over it.

Then the road lay between two great waterfalls. It took brave men to force their way through the torrent, jostled and bruised by falling stones. There was nothing cowardly about the seven, however, and they were quick as well.

The pass led on and up to a narrow ledge no wider than a man's hand and over this they had to walk one at a time, without falling into the gorges on either side. This too they successfully accomplished.

169

At last they came to the sea's edge where they found a canoe equipped with seven paddles. Munagesunook lay far off in the distance, a tiny speck on the water, but the waves were high and the men tarried hoping the storm would abate, but it continued worse than ever.

"We must risk it!"

So, launching themselves on the wild sea, they set out for the island, straining over the paddles. Nearing the opposite shore, a great wave struck and the canoe capsized, leaving the seven to swim the rest of the way to shore. They reached it at last, half-drowned but alive.

"Well done!" There stood the Master, gazing at them with approval. "Come with me."

Glooscap led them to his great lodge where they found handsome doeskin garments laid out for them. Freshly clothed, they were invited to seats in the higher part of the wigwam and their genial host passed round pipe and tobacco. Then Noogumee came in and put a pot of water on the fire and presently the boy, Marten, brought an old bare beaver bone to her and she scraped some of it into the kettle. The seven looked at each other, thinking they were due for a poor meal. But, as the water began to boil, the scrapings thickened up and the kettle was soon full of fat pieces of flesh, giving off a wonderful aroma—and they saw Glooscap laughing at them. Then they knew this must be the Master's magic food, which never grew less no matter how much one ate of it.

After the meal, they took it in turn to tell stories and, when all were relaxed and happy, Glooscap came to the main business.

"Now tell me, each of you, what is the chief wish of your heart?"

The first man, who was honest and simple and of but little account among his neighbors because he was such a poor hunter, said, "Master, I would like to be expert at finding game. I don't want more than I need, just enough to feed myself and my family and perhaps my neighbors when they are in need." So Glooscap gave him a magic flute which had the power to persuade animals to follow the one who played it. "You must promise, however," said the Lord of Men and Beasts, "not to play it until you reach home." And the man promised.

The second man, who had no thought in his mind save pleasure, asked for the love of many women. "I care not how many, so that there are enough and a few to spare!" At this, the Great Chief looked displeased, yet he produced a small bag which the man had to promise not to open until he reached home.

The third man, a gay and handsome fellow, had his heart set on making people laugh, so that he would always win a welcome at every lodge. He asked for the knack of making a certain quaint and marvelous sound, frequent in those times, so that those who heard it must always burst out laughing. Wondering why a man would come so far at such a cost for so trifling a wish, Glooscap never-theless kept his promise and gave the young man a magic root. "Promise you will not eat of it until you are back in your own village." And the young man promised.

The fourth man asked for a medicine to cure him of all diseases. "Only enough," he said, "for myself." The Great Chief made no comment but gave him a small package with the usual injunction, and this man also promised.

The fifth man wished he might be able to see his ene-mies before they saw him—"so that I can kill them before they kill me." Saddened by this wish too, Glooscap never-theless gave the man a small box with the usual caution —"Do not open the box until the end of your journey." And this man also promised.

The sixth man was vain of his looks and wore bark in his moccasins to make himself taller. He wore also a turkey-tail feather in his hairstring, which made him seem taller still, and what this Indian wanted most was to be taller than all others in the land. He too received his box and promised to restrain his impatience to open it.

The seventh man was one of those who think themselves finer and better than ordinary folk and he wished he might outlive all his companions, so the world would not be deprived of him too soon. He too was given a box and gave a promise in return.

And now after supplying the seven with food for the return journey, Glooscap called Bootup the whale and had him carry the men to the mainland on his back. There they found seven *luskuns*— a *luskun* being a piece of bark scratched with trail instructions put there by Glooscap to show each the quickest and safest way home to his own village.

Going back was therefore easy.

The first man, who had asked to excel at hunting, kept his promise, confident that from now on he and his family would have enough to eat, and so it was. There was always venison in his lodge and enough to spare for the neighbors, and this man was content all his days.

The second man, who loved women, was filled with anxiety about his gift and could not wait to get home. He opened the box and at once there flew out hundreds of white doves which, as they clustered about him, turned into girls with black eyes and long flowing hair. They were so many, he begged them to stand off a little and give him air, but they would not listen. They clustered closer and ever closer until he sank down under their weight and suffocated. What became of the girls, no man knows.

The third man, who wanted to make people laugh, walked gaily along until he suddenly thought to himself that he would just try Glooscap's medicine to make sure it worked. He ate a bit of the root and at once heard himself utter the magic sound to perfection. He walked on, repeating the sound over and over, making the valley ring with it, until at last, growing hungry, he began to stalk a fat young caribou. Just as he was about to draw bow, the magic sound burst forth and the caribou bounded out of range. Now the young man tried with all his might to repress the sound, but always it issued forth at the most inopportune moment. Seeing that at this rate he would soon starve to death, the young man anticipated matters by killing himself there and then.

The fourth man, who had asked for a medicine to cure all his diseases, went his way resolved for his health's sake to keep his promise. Then it occurred to him that if Glooscap had made a mistake in his prescription, it would be a long and dangerous road back to correct the error. Better to make sure before he went farther, so he opened the box and that which was in it fell out and spread like water, then dried away like mist in the sun.

The fifth man, who wished to see his enemies before they saw him, thought he had better be ready in case he met one of them unexpectedly, so while still a long way from home he opened his box. The contents flew up in his eyes and blinded him, and never after that did he see enemies, friends, or anything else.

The sixth man, who was vain of his looks and wished to be tall, also yielded to temptation, but on opening his box felt his feet sink in the earth where they were held fast. Now he was a pine tree with his head rising high above all the trees in the forest, turkey-tail topknot waving in the breeze.

175

And the seventh, who wanted to outlive everyone, having come to the top of a high hill, reasoned that ordinary rules did not apply to him. He opened the box and at once he became a cedar tree—a tree all bent and twisted by the hill's high winds, too knotty for lumber, too hard to burn, safe to outlive everyone but Glooscap.

Now the Lord of Men and Beasts, knowing all as all happened, sighed for the foolishness of men. He had been mistaken. There were still monsters in the world—monsters of greed and cruelty, of selfishness and silliness, of vanity and bad faith. These, unfortunately, were in man's own nature and could only be cast out by man himself. His people had knowledge, but not wisdom. He knew now what he must do.

He sent Kweemoo to gather all the Wabanaki to a feast on the shore of Minas Basin. They came from all the tribes of men and creatures and there was a great number, feeding joyously on Glooscap's bounty. They were merry together all day, but when the light began to leave the sky the Master rose and a hush fell over the assembly.

"I am going away," he said. "I must leave you."

A moment while they hoped they had misunderstood him, then a wail broke forth. The Great Chief held up his hand.

"It must be," he said. "Birds, if kept in the nest too long, will not learn to fly. Nor can a people grow if, like children, they are always under protection and obedience."

"Stay with us yet a while," they begged, but the Master shook his head.

"I must go to the land behind the clouds to make arrows for the day of the final great battle between Good and Evil. On that day, Malsum will rise with Lox on his right hand and all the monsters of evil behind him. All you who have learned wisdom meanwhile will stand with me on that day, and if we are strong we will defeat the Wolf and his army."

He turned to Noogumee, his housekeeper, and put his amethyst beads about her neck. The white hair turned raven black, all her wrinkles faded, and she was lovely. "Your name is Oona now. I give you youth and forgetfulness." And Oona walked away into the arms of her people without a backward glance.

A touch on the magic belt and Marten alike was deprived of the pain of memory. The little *megumoowesoo* ran off smiling to join the halfway people.

Now Glooscap took his empty kettle from the fire and flung it into Minas Basin where it landed bottom up and became a spruce-crowned isle which to this day the Indians call *ooteomul*, "his kettle." His dogs, Day and Night, he turned into rocks at the foot of Blomidon to wait his return. To the loon he gave his freedom.

Then the Lord of Men and Beasts threw into the water a stick which turned into a great canoe packed with supplies for a journey. "Hold to your courage," he shouted.

"That you will need most of all!" And springing into his canoe, he thrust off from shore.

A deep sigh passed over the gathering. Glooscap was leaving them. Heavy-hearted, they watched his canoe move rapidly over the sea and disappear into the western sky. Even after they saw him no more, their eyes blinded by the setting sun, they could hear his voice singing his farewell song. The sound grew fainter and fainter and at last wholly died away.

Then all nature began to mourn. Kookoogwes the owl sighed "koo-koo-koo" which means "Oh, I am sorry," and this the owls still cry. The loons went restlessly up and down the world asking for their Master, wailing because they found him not, as they do to this day. Men and beasts could no longer speak to each other nor understand each other, and that is the way it is now.

The Wabanaki have learned to live without Glooscap for the present. Life is hard and may be harder, they say, but they are practicing to be strong and wise, for one day Glooscap will come again. Then they will stand on his side in the great battle, the arrows will fly, and their enemies will drop like rain!

And so—*kespeadooksit*—the stories end.

The Author

KAY HILL is a Nova Scotian and lives in a village near the mouth of Halifax Harbour, not far from the place where Glooscap had his lodge on Blomidon. A writer for radio and television, she was invited to adapt the legends of the Wabanaki for CBC Television, and the resulting programs drew thousands of enthusiastic letters, from adults as well as children.

Miss Hill's most recent book, AND TOMORROW THE STARS: The Story of John Cabot, won the 1968 medal for Best Children's book in English, awarded by the Canadian Association of Children's Librarians. She is also the author of scores of adult plays for radio and television, as well as several stage plays.

The Illustrator

JOHN HAMBERGER has illustrated over a dozen children's books, among them Kay Hill's BADGER, THE MISCHIEF MAKER and five of his own picture books, notably HAZEL WAS AN ONLY PET and THE PEACOCK WHO LOST HIS TAIL.

Born on Long Island, Mr. Hamberger attended the School of Visual Arts in New York City. He is a member of the Society of Animal Artists, and his paintings are on permanent exhibit in The American Museum of Natural History's new "Hall of Ocean Life." He and his wife and young son live in Manhattan, but have a farm in Pennsylvania where he paints and studies wildlife.